TRAUMA

Trauma has become a catchword of our time and a central category in contemporary theory and criticism. In this illuminating and accessible volume, Lucy Bond and Stef Craps:

- provide an account of the history of the concept of trauma from the late nineteenth century to the present day
- examine debates around the term in their historical and cultural contexts
- trace the origins and growth of literary trauma theory
- introduce the reader to key thinkers in the field
- explore important issues and tensions in the study of trauma as a cultural phenomenon
- outline and assess recent critiques and revisions of cultural trauma research

Trauma is an essential guide to a rich and vibrant area of literary and cultural inquiry.

Lucy Bond is a principal lecturer in English literature at the University of Westminster, UK.

Stef Craps is a professor of English literature at Ghent University, Belgium.

THE NEW CRITICAL IDIOM

SERIES EDITOR: JOHN DRAKAKIS, UNIVERSITY OF STIRLING

The New Critical Idiom is an invaluable series of introductory guides to today's critical terminology. Each book:

- provides a handy, explanatory guide to the use (and abuse) of the term;
- offers an original and distinctive overview by a leading literary and cultural critic;
- relates the term to the larger field of cultural representation.

With a strong emphasis on clarity, lively debate and the widest possible breadth of examples, The New Critical Idiom is an indispensable approach to key topics in literary studies.

Spatiality by Robert T. Tally Jr
Epic by Paul Innes
Grotesque by Justin D Edwards and Rune Graulund
Fairy Tale by Andrew Teverson
Translation by Susan Bassnett
Gothic—Second edition by Fred Botting
Narrative—Second edition by Paul Cobley
Comedy—Second edition by Andrew Stott
Genre—Second edition by John Frow
Colonialism/Postcolonialism—Third edition by Ania Loomba
Adaptation and Appropriation—second edition by Julie Sanders
The Aphorism and Other Short Forms Ben Grant by Ben Grant
Modernism—Third edition by Peter Childs
Reception by Ika Willis
The Sublime—Second edition by Philip Shaw
Satire by John T. Gilmore
Race by Martin Orkin with Alexa Alice Joubin
Trauma by Stef Craps and Lucy Bond
Children's Literature by Carrie Hintz
Pastoral–Second edition by Terry Gifford

For more information about this series, please visit: www.routledge.com/literature/series/SE0155

TRAUMA

Lucy Bond and Stef Craps

LONDON AND NEW YORK

First published 2020
by Routledge
2 Park Square, Milton Park, Abingdon, Oxon OX14 4RN

and by Routledge
52 Vanderbilt Avenue, New York, NY 10017

Routledge is an imprint of the Taylor & Francis Group, an informa business

British Library Cataloguing in Publication Data
A catalogue record for this book is available from the British Library

Library of Congress Cataloging-in-Publication Data
A catalog record has been requested for this book

ISBN: 978-0-415-54041-4 (hbk)
ISBN: 978-0-415-54042-1 (pbk)
ISBN: 978-0-203-38306-3 (ebk)

Typeset in Times New Roman
by Taylor & Francis Books

Printed and bound by CPI Group (UK) Ltd, Croydon, CR0 4YY

For Alex, Karen, and Amber

Contents

Acknowledgements viii
Series editor's preface ix

Introduction: Not even past **1**

1 The history of trauma **12**

2 Words for wounds **45**

3 Trauma theories **73**

4 The future of trauma **103**

Conclusion: The limits of trauma **132**

Glossary **143**

Bibliography 152
Index 166

Acknowledgements

This book has been a long time in the making, and we have incurred debts of gratitude to many people and institutions along the way. We want to thank our colleagues in the School of Humanities at the University of Westminster and the Department of Literary Studies and the Cultural Memory Studies Initiative at Ghent University for their valuable input. We are grateful also to Michael Rothberg and Jessica Rapson for their support from the outset of this project. Moreover, we wish to thank Ghent University and the Flemish Research Council (FWO) for the sabbatical leave that allowed Stef to write part of the book, and Roger Luckhurst and Katia Pizzi for hosting him as a visiting scholar at Birkbeck and the School of Advanced Study, University of London during that time. We want to particularly acknowledge our students, on various courses we have taught at Westminster, Ghent, and UCLA over the years, for helping us think through many of the issues explored here. Polly Dodson and Zoe Meyer have been extremely patient and encouraging editors, as has the series editor, John Drakakis. Many thanks to all three of them. Most of all, though, we owe a debt of gratitude to our partners, Alex Hensby and Karen Van Holm, for cheering us on during the writing of this book, and to Stef's daughter Amber, for providing welcome distractions. The book is dedicated to them. Our hope for it is that, in some small way, it will help readers navigate and make sense of the troubled world in which we live, which is haunted not only by the spectres of past atrocities but also by the ghosts of devastations that are ongoing or yet to come.

Series editor's preface

The New Critical Idiom is a series of introductory books which seeks to extend the lexicon of literary terms, in order to address the radical changes which have taken place in the study of literature during the last decades of the twentieth century. The aim is to provide clear, well-illustrated accounts of the full range of terminology currently in use, and to evolve histories of its changing usage.

The current state of the discipline of literary studies is one where there is considerable debate concerning basic questions of terminology. This involves, among other things, the boundaries which distinguish the literary from the non-literary; the position of literature within the larger sphere of culture; the relationship between literatures of different cultures; and questions concerning the relation of literary to other cultural forms within the context of interdisciplinary studies.

It is clear that the field of literary criticism and theory is a dynamic and heterogeneous one. The present need is for individual volumes on terms which combine clarity of exposition with an adventurousness of perspective and a breadth of application. Each volume will contain as part of its apparatus some indication of the direction in which the definition of particular terms is likely to move, as well as expanding the disciplinary boundaries within which some of these terms have been traditionally contained. This will involve some re-situation of terms within the larger field of cultural representation, and will introduce examples from the area of film and the modern media in addition to examples from a variety of literary texts.

INTRODUCTION: NOT EVEN PAST

On 18 March 2008, Democratic Illinois Senator Barack Obama gave a speech at the Constitution Center in Philadelphia. The address was intended to cool the controversy that had erupted in the wake of an *ABC News* investigation into the sermons of Reverend Jeremiah Wright, who had repeatedly denounced the United States for its long-standing racial violence against people of colour. In one excerpt from 2003, Wright raged, 'God damn America for treating our citizens as less than human. God damn America for as long as she acts like she is God and she is supreme' (qtd in Ross and El-Buri 2008). Even more contentiously, Wright argued that America's own 'terrorism' in Hiroshima and Nagaski, more than fifty years earlier, had led to the terrorist attacks of 11 September 2001. Obama acknowledged that Wright, who was his former pastor and an unpaid campaign adviser, had made a 'profound mistake' in his divisive claims. However, he cautioned, 'race is an issue that I believe this nation cannot afford to ignore'; 'Understanding this reality requires a reminder of how we arrived at this point. As William Faulkner once wrote, "The past isn't dead and buried. In fact, it isn't even past"' (2008).

While Obama slightly misquoted Faulkner—the correct lines, taken from the 1951 novel *Requiem for a Nun,* read, 'The past is never dead. It's not even past'—we share this sentiment. The past is alive in the present, and its legacies continue to resonate in complex and controversial ways. While the traces of the past are all around us, the memories that exert the deepest pull on our emotions are often those connected to violent histories. Traumatic experiences leave deep scars that can remain unresolved for decades, generations, even centuries. Being bound to the past while struggling to overcome it is no short order: as Obama argues, the challenge is to find a means of 'embracing the burdens of our past without becoming victims of our past' (2008). His Philadelphia speech charts America's evolution from European colony to global superpower, citing the War of Independence, the Civil War, slavery, lynching, Jim Crow, the Great Depression, the Second World War, the AIDS epidemic, the O. J. Simpson trial, 9/11, the 'War on Terror', Hurricane Katrina, the healthcare crisis, and climate change as definitive moments in the nation's journey. In so doing, it casts American history as a melting pot of traumas, some past, some present, and some still unfolding, but all of them active and enduring.

As Obama suggests, violent histories are nothing new. However, the development of a diagnostic language able to identify them as 'traumatic' is surprisingly recent. According to the *Oxford English Dictionary* (2000), the first recorded mention of 'trauma' (which comes from the Greek word for wound) in English occurred in 1693, when the second edition of *Blanchard's Physical Dictionary* defined it as 'a wound from an external cause'. Throughout the seventeenth and eighteenth centuries, trauma was understood as a physical injury. It was not until the late nineteenth century, when the enormous transformations of industrial modernity exposed people to new and hitherto unimagined dangers, that the notion of *psychological* trauma began to take root. As Google's Ngram viewer (an online search engine that tracks the frequency with which a term has been found in print between 1500 and 2008) reveals, the rise of trauma has been meteoric. References to trauma increased 3,600% between 1880 and the end of the First World War in 1918, and a massive 31,000% between 1880 and the highest number of annual mentions in 2004. As we will argue throughout this book, the reasons for this trauma boom are complicated: it is not that our lives have become inherently more traumatic, but that we have found new ways to categorize, represent, and exploit distressing experiences.

Today, trauma is big business. It is the focus of numerous novels, artworks, films, songs, and video games. A trauma aesthetic has come to dominate the architecture of monuments and museums, from Maya Lin's iconic Vietnam Veterans' Memorial on the Mall in Washington, DC to Peter Eisenman's Memorial to the Murdered Jews of Europe in central Berlin. A thriving trauma industry informs our leisure and consumer choices: dark tourist locations such as concentration camps, battlefields, plantations, and prisons draw millions of visitors each year, and their gift shops boast huge turnovers. Fashion retailers have also sought to capitalize on trauma's commercial potential: in 2014, the British clothing chain Zara released a line of striped children's pyjamas reminiscent of the outfits worn by prisoners in Auschwitz, complete with a gold star on the breast pocket. Meanwhile, online sales of official and unofficial Black Lives Matter merchandise have helped transform a grassroots movement that campaigns against violence and systemic racism towards black Americans into a globally recognizable brand. Yet, the motivations that underlie the marketing and consumption of trauma differ widely. While wearing a Black Lives Matter T-shirt might legitimately be seen as a positive form of political engagement, it is more difficult to understand what might reasonably encourage a parent to purchase a pair of 'Holocaust pyjamas' for their child. Such differences illustrate the importance of exploring the differential ethical and ideological dynamics at work in the trauma industry.

This is equally the case in mainstream political culture, where groups at both ends of the spectrum have used the rhetoric of trauma to frame their demands for recognition and rights. In the late 1970s and early 1980s, the language of trauma provided a vehicle for feminist and gay rights activists to articulate their experiences of marginalization and abuse. While the predominantly liberal discourses associated with such identity politics have historically found little sympathy from conservative campaigners, more recently the narrative of victimhood has taken a surprising ideological turn, as alt-right groups in Europe and America have sought to emphasize their own sense of disenfranchisement. The success of today's political movements, left and right, is often premised upon activists' ability to exploit a competitive politics of grief that sees claims for recognition played out in raced, gendered, classed, or sexualized terms. As Terri Tomsky has noted, such zero-sum debates constitute a 'trauma economy' in which memories are mediated by 'economic, cultural, discursive, and political structures that guide, enable and ultimately institutionalize the representation, travel and attention to certain traumas' (2011: 53). So central has the idea of trauma become to questions about identity, inclusion, and belonging that critics have argued that we are living in a trauma culture, defined by a valorization of victimhood (Farrell 1998; Luckhurst 2003; Luckhurst 2008; Kaplan 2005).

Yet, for all its ubiquity, the definition of trauma remains unstable. The transition from professional to popular discourse has arguably led to a loss of specificity in its meaning and application. As we will see, such changeability has characterized the term throughout its history. So how should we conceptualize this most mutable pathology? Richard Crownshaw notes that, despite ongoing debate, critics generally agree that 'trauma is that which defies witnessing, cognition, conscious recall and representation' (2010: 4). Drawing upon the Freudian model of trauma and the more recent categorization of post-traumatic stress disorder (PTSD), both explored in Chapter 1, most cultural and literary theories position trauma as a *belated* response to an overwhelming event too shattering to be processed as it occurs. Traumatic memories are repressed as they are formed, leaving them unavailable to conscious recall; subsequently, they recur in various displaced ways, as hallucinations, flashbacks, or nightmares. When the traumatic experience returns, unbidden, to consciousness, the sudden collision of past and present 'violently opens passageways between systems that were once discrete, making unforeseen connections that distress or confound' (Luckhurst 2008: 3). Trauma is both highly resistant to articulation and wildly generative of narratives that seek to explicate the 'unclaimed' originary experience (Caruth 1996). As Roger Luckhurst suggests, trauma 'also appears worryingly transmissible: it leaks between mental and physical symptoms, between patients … between patients and doctors via the mysterious processes of transference or suggestion, and between victims and their listeners or viewers' (2008: 3).

Trauma, then, is slippery: blurring the boundaries between mind and body, memory and forgetting, speech and silence. It traverses the internal and the external, the private and the public, the individual and the collective. Trauma is dynamic: its parameters are endlessly shifting as it moves across disciplines and institutions, ages and cultures. Trauma is contested: its rhetoric, its origins, its symptoms, and its treatment have been subject to more than 150 years of controversy and debate. As Ruth Leys contends, '[t]he history of trauma itself is marked by an alternation between episodes of remembering and forgetting, as the experiences of one generation of psychiatrists have been neglected only to be revived at a later time' (2000: 15). Judith Herman consequently suggests that the intellectual history of trauma is *traumatized*, marked by 'episodic amnesia', 'periodically forgotten', and 'periodically reclaimed' (1992b: 7). For all of the above reasons, Mark Micale and Paul Lerner assert that trauma 'is nothing if not elastic' (2001: 20).

With a full awareness of these complexities, this book examines various conceptions of trauma in the light of their historical, institutional, and cultural contexts as we explore how trauma has moved from an object of medical and legal concern in nineteenth-century Europe to a central facet of global culture today. This is not a clinical history: we do not aim to offer a detailed account of changing psychiatric approaches to trauma. Nor have we written an exhaustive genealogy of the historical events and cultural media most associated with traumatic memories. Rather, we will highlight some of the most important developments in trauma studies, focusing in particular on the evolution of literary trauma theory. There are significant overlaps between the fields of literature and trauma. As Anne Whitehead establishes, '[t]he rise of trauma theory has provided novelists with new ways of conceptualising trauma and has shifted attention away from the question of what is remembered of the past to how and why it is remembered' (2004: 3). The widespread desire 'among various cultural groups to represent or make visible specific historical instances of trauma has given rise to numerous important works of contemporary fiction' (2004: 3). Whitehead points, in particular, to the work of the late Toni Morrison and her ongoing attempts to reckon with the trauma of slavery in novels such as *Beloved* (1987) and *Jazz* (1992). As Whitehead observes, 'fiction itself has been marked or changed by its encounter with trauma. Novelists have frequently found that the impact of trauma can only adequately be represented by mimicking its forms and symptoms, so that temporality and chronology collapse, and narratives are characterised by repetition and indirection' (2004: 3). The result of this encounter, she suggests, is the new genre of 'trauma fiction', represented by authors such as W. G. Sebald, Caryl Phillips, and Anne Michaels. While a growing number of literary critics have become interested in the study of trauma fiction, meanwhile, contemporary authors have in turn been influenced by psychiatric and psychoanalytical paradigms of trauma. Pat Barker's *Regeneration* trilogy (1991–1995; see Barker 2013), for example, examines the treatment of shell-shocked soldiers, including the poets Siegfried Sassoon and Wilfred Owen, at Craiglockhart Hospital in Edinburgh during the First World War.

While, as we will see, the boundaries of trauma fiction have been questioned and a wider range of texts is currently being studied than was the case during the early days of literary trauma theory, trauma is rarely projected far back in time. Literature has represented human suffering, whether real or imagined, for as long as it has existed, but trauma relates specifically to a psychical condition connected to, and recognized after, the onset of Western modernity. Moreover, the thematization and formal emulation of the 'unspeakability' of trauma appears to be a modern innovation. As a general rule, pre-modern narrative forms such as ancient Greek tragedy do not focus on the impossibility of articulating experiences that are unavailable to conscious memory the way works of trauma literature do. The latter also tend to eschew the kind of cathartic redemption often embraced by tragedy and its theorists, most famously the Greek philosopher Aristotle, who argued in his *Poetics* that a good tragedy should incite 'pity and fear' in its audience. By contrast, modern trauma writers and critics typically discourage adopting a vicarious relationship to the suffering of others, regarding it as appropriative and unethical. Rather than aiming for comprehensive coverage of conceptions and expressions of human suffering throughout history, therefore, this book focuses its critical energies on examining manifestations, theorizations, and representations of trauma from the nineteenth century to the present.

Chapter 1 traces the relationship between trauma and modernity, arguing that the intellectual history of trauma cannot be viewed in isolation from the social, economic, political, and cultural contexts in which it is embedded and with which it interacts. We begin by exploring how studies of railway and industrial accidents in Britain and Germany in the mid-to-late nineteenth century took the first step in repositioning trauma from a physical wound to a psychological injury. Next, we examine how early clinical research on nervous disorders gradually shifted from an interest in physiological models of hysteria towards a more psychodynamic approach to trauma, focusing on the seminal work of Jean-Martin Charcot, Pierre Janet, and Sigmund Freud. Third, we consider how the massive psychological impact of the First World War was responded to in different national contexts, highlighting the ways in which military and political interests affected the codification and reception of mental illness. As we will see, the link between trauma and warfare was reinforced throughout the twentieth century, most explicitly in the aftermath of the Vietnam War, when the American Psychiatric Association (APA) officially recognized PTSD for the first time in the third edition of its *Diagnostic and Statistical Manual of Mental Disorders* (American Psychiatric Association 1980). The APA's classification of PTSD gave medical legitimacy to trauma patients, raising the public profile of the pathology. Finally, the chapter addresses the migration of the concept of trauma from psychiatric discourse into contemporary 'wound culture' (Seltzer 1997), a society obsessed with displaying its traumas.

Chapter 2 examines how trauma functions in literary and cultural theory. We trace the interest paid by literary and cultural scholars to issues of trauma over the last three decades back to the work of Theodor Adorno, particularly to his famous claim that 'to write poetry after Auschwitz is barbaric' (1981: 34) and his later statement that 'literature must resist this verdict' (1980: 188). We illustrate how the imperative to represent the unrepresentable, which Adorno set art and cultural criticism, also informs the work of George Steiner, Maurice Blanchot, and Jean-François Lyotard. We go on to explain why in the 1990s a number of literary theorists who share a background in deconstruction—Cathy Caruth, Shoshana Felman, and Geoffrey Hartman—turned their attention to this paradoxical task, becoming leading figures in cultural trauma theory. Offering a brief survey of paradigm shifts in literary studies over the last quarter of the twentieth century, we describe how deconstruction went from being the dominant paradigm in the 1970s and early 1980s to being increasingly maligned and marginalized in the course of the 1980s. Accused of being indifferent and irrelevant to history, politics, and ethics because of its alleged excessive fixation on language, deconstruction was eclipsed by various new paradigms that purported to be more attentive to such 'real-world' issues, including new historicism, cultural materialism, cultural studies, postcolonialism, feminism, and Marxism. We argue that trauma theory as developed by Caruth, Felman, Hartman, and their colleague Dori Laub in the early 1990s can be understood as an attempt to reclaim an ethical space for deconstruction by stressing its usefulness as a critical tool for interrogating the relationship between referentiality and historical violence.

Chapter 3 shows the range and heterogeneity of cultural trauma theory by exploring some important issues and tensions that have marked the field over the past several decades. We discuss how the work of founding figures like Caruth, Felman, Hartman, and Laub has been revised and expanded by later theorists, looking particularly at the possibility of collective or cultural trauma and the debates surrounding secondary or vicarious witnessing. We begin by considering the difference between structural and historical trauma, which is often overlooked in early trauma theory. As Dominick LaCapra argues, structural trauma results from a foundational absence and thus cannot be overcome. By contrast, historical trauma relates to a specific instance of loss and carries the possibility of being worked through in time, allowing a productive re-engagement with the future. We then move on to examine the critical tensions that have emerged over the transmission of trauma, looking at the possibility that traumatic memories may be passed across generations and may even be assumed by people with no direct connection to the original experience. We assess the changing media through which secondary traumatization has been said to occur, including the extent to which evolving media and digital technologies have shaped the transmission of trauma since the turn of the new millennium. Finally, we turn to the idea of collective trauma, which has proved particularly contentious in recent scholarship. We highlight the differences between theorists who understand trauma to occur in collectives in much the same ways as it does in individuals and those who understand collective or cultural trauma as a social construct.

Chapter 4 acquaints the reader with four of the latest developments in cultural trauma research by outlining and assessing various critiques and revisions intended to expand, reorient, or otherwise advance the field. First, we highlight the blind-spots that have led canonical trauma theory to marginalize the experiences of non-Western and minority groups by prioritizing 'Western' atrocities such as the Holocaust and 9/11. In an attempt to redress this imbalance, a number of scholars have argued that the parameters of cultural trauma studies must be widened to address other traumatic experiences such as those associated with slavery, colonialism, apartheid, Partition, and the Stolen Generations. A related strand of criticism, spearheaded by Michael Rothberg's influential work on 'multidirectional memory' (2009), has called for a comparative approach to memory that views historical violence through a cross-cultural framework. The second new direction of cultural trauma research that we focus upon is a tendency to study texts—popular, realist, or indigenous literature—that deviate from the modernist aesthetic of fragmentation and discontinuity, adherence to which has long been seen as a requirement for entry into the canon of valued trauma literature. Moreover, more and more attention is being paid to the representation of traumatic experiences in media other than literature, particularly photography, film, theatre, and video games. We suggest that this extension of trauma theory in the direction of visual culture is unsurprising given the central role accorded to intrusive images in dominant models of trauma. The third development we explore is a critical shift from prioritizing the experience of the victim to exploring that of the perpetrator: while testimonial and literary work by and about victims has received a great deal of critical and scholarly attention, the dearth of research on representations of perpetrators has only just begun to be addressed. Finally, we look at recent debates surrounding the psychological impact of climate change and other forms of 'pre-traumatic experience' that challenge established models of temporality and causality.

The conclusion offers some final remarks on the benefits as well as the limits of cultural trauma research. Trauma studies can provide a basis for cultural and political critique by fostering attunement to previously unheard suffering, we argue, but an obsession with traumatic histories threatens to displace other kinds of memory, including memories of non-traumatizing injustice and of collective mobilization, with potentially depoliticizing results. While the field of trauma studies continues to evolve, tapping into new and fertile areas of research, it would be prudent to guard against overreach and overambition.

Examining key developments in the theorization of trauma over the past 150 years, with an emphasis on its role in literary and cultural scholarship, this book aims to provide insight into the ways in which the past is 'not even past'. Writing in the *Guardian* in the run-up to the third official Holocaust Memorial Day in 2003, the British historian David Cesarani contended that there was 'no truer' reflection of Faulkner's words than the legacies of 'Nazi persecution and mass murder of the Jews between 1933 and 1945, and the "racial state" that Hitler created in Germany and nearly imposed on the whole of Europe'. 'After more than half a century', Cesarani asserted, 'racism, xenophobia and political intolerance remain potent forces throughout Europe' (2002). The same, of course, is true today, as the resurgence of the far right and the rise of neo-Nazism across Europe and America make clear. However, Cesarani saw in Holocaust Memorial Day more than 'a simple act of piety: it is designed to be a springboard for positive action'. In recognizing how the events of the Second World War continue to haunt the present, 'communities have discovered former refugees in their midst and unearthed histories of local activism on behalf of those seeking a haven from oppression'. In turn, 'these memories have provoked questions about the way British society and the state behaved in the 1930s, and inevitably, how we act today towards refugees and asylum seekers' (2002).

Cesarani argued that by encouraging wider cultural recognition of the intimate relationship between the past and the present, events like Holocaust Memorial Day have the potential to challenge ongoing forms of violence and injustice. In his Philadelphia address, Obama similarly urged that confronting the 'racial stalemate we've been stuck in for years' could lead the United States to 'a more perfect union' (2008). The presentness of the past, then, need not be a uniquely bad thing: reflexively addressed, it holds the potential to generate transhistorical and transcultural forms of empathy and understanding. However, this would require a collective willingness to adopt a critical perspective on history, and to acknowledge different forms of traumatic experience without appropriating them. As Obama cautioned in his famous speech on race, we must 'find the common stake we all have in one another, and let our politics reflect that spirit as well' (2008). This must surely be the goal of any truly ethical culture of trauma.

1

THE HISTORY OF TRAUMA

Critics have often connected the origins of the trauma paradigm to the onset of Western modernity. As Roger Luckhurst contends, 'trauma is a concept that can only emerge within modernity, … as an effect of the rise, in the nineteenth century, of the technical and statistical society that can generate, multiply and quantify the "shocks" of modern life' (2008: 19). The growing interest in nervous disorders in the mid-to-late nineteenth century can be directly traced to a number of related social, economic, political, and technological developments that contributed to a massive transformation of everyday life. The sheer scale and speed with which Western nations modernized produced a widespread sense of insecurity, as 'the excesses of mechanized work, travel, and warfare', along with increasingly 'unstable social and cultural systems', converged to reveal the modern world as 'an open, mass, secular, dynamic, heterogeneous, capitalist, and liberal-democratic culture with all its confusions, complexities, and incoherences' (Micale 2001: 139). Throughout Europe and America, growing public and professional fascination with nervous disorders was linked to sweeping changes in socio-cultural worldviews, catalysed by the rise of empire; the spread of socialism, feminism, anarchism, and secularism; and processes of urbanization, industrialization, technologization, and democratization.

The emergence of the trauma paradigm was thus 'simultaneously responsive to and constitutive of "modernity"' (Micale and Lerner 2001: 22). Two contemporaneous developments brought trauma to the forefront of public consciousness in the late nineteenth century: first, significant advancements in the mental sciences repositioned nervous disorders as the product of psychical, rather than physical, causes; second, the increasing mechanization of industrial society transformed conventional modes of travel, labour, warfare, and leisure. As Mark Micale and Paul Lerner contend, nineteenth-century Europe 'saw the growth of technological modernity parallel to the formation of the first organized and systematized means for studying its consequences on the human psyche', and these 'two developments occurred in a … self-reinforcing manner; together they gave birth to the medical and cultural engagement with mental trauma' (2001: 11).

Emphasizing the link between processes of historical change and developments in scientific knowledge, this chapter positions psychiatric accounts of trauma in relation to the advent of 'concurrent modernities' (Micale 2001: 139), stretching from the mid-nineteenth to the late twentieth centuries. Conceptions of trauma vary dramatically from nation to nation, decade to decade, and clinician to clinician, making it necessary to consider attitudes towards nervous disorders within the specific historical, cultural, and institutional contexts of their emergence. Since the mid-nineteenth century, understandings of trauma have remained consistently in flux, shifting in response to the varied approaches of mental health professionals (neurocognitive, psychiatric, psychodynamic, etc.), who have differed significantly over which groups or individuals (in classed, raced, and gendered terms) might prove more predisposed to nervous disorders of one kind or another, and which mode of clinical treatment might prove most appropriate to the recovery of these patients (hypnosis, medication, electric shocks, psychotherapy, etc.). The terminology in which trauma has been couched has also proven remarkably fluid, and the label has functioned as an umbrella for a number of different but related pathologies (including, in the nineteenth century, hysteria, railway spine, traumatic neurosis, and neurasthenia, and, more recently, shell-shock, war neurosis, combat fatigue, PTSD, and Gulf War Syndrome) whose visibility has waxed and waned according to disciplinary fashions and political necessity.

Such developments reveal how changing socio-political norms and values inflect conceptualization of nervous and mental disorders. Because clinical understandings of trauma are at least partially socially constructed, what counts as trauma in one context may not be recognized as such in another. Approaches to trauma are culturally and historically contingent, respondent to both the changing environments that give rise to them and the cultural, scientific, legal, and political power structures that allow them to exist. Interrogating such ambiguities, this chapter examines conceptions of trauma in different clinical, cultural, and historical contexts. The first section foregrounds the relationship between trauma and the new technologies of modernity, focusing particularly on John Erichsen's work on railway spine in the UK and Hermann Oppenheim's theories of traumatic neuroses from industrial accidents in Germany in the mid-to-late nineteenth century. The second section examines the origins of hysteria in the research of three seminal figures in early psychiatric practice: Jean-Martin Charcot, Pierre Janet, and Sigmund Freud. The third section explores the intimate connection between trauma and warfare that was forged during the First World War, looking at different approaches to the psychiatric treatment of soldiers in Germany, Italy, the UK, and the US. The fourth part of the chapter examines the emergence of a master paradigm of trauma, post-traumatic stress disorder (PTSD), in America in the aftermath of the Vietnam War, and the final part considers the evolution of a broader trauma culture at the end of the twentieth century.

THE PUZZLE OF RAILWAY SPINE AND THE PERILS OF INDUSTRIALIZATION

The nineteenth century brought human life into ever more intimate contact with technology. Central to this process was the development of an expansive network of railways across the Western world, which, from 1830 onwards, transformed the experience of time and space. As Christian Wolmar notes, '[t]raveling by train was an utterly novel experience' (2007: 43) that 'demonstrated how the Industrial Revolution was accelerating the rate of social change. Indeed, the railways were the greatest product of the Revolution, and its major driver' (2007: 54). However, alongside the undoubted advantages of faster and more reliable travel, the expansion of the railways exposed Victorians to new forms of risk. As Ralph Harrington argues, from the 1840s to the 1860s, the growing number of casualties resulting from railway accidents created 'a uniquely sensational and public demonstration of the price which [technology] demanded—violence, destruction, terror, and trauma', embodying and symbolizing 'many of the age's apprehensions about progress, technological development, and modernity' (2001: 31).

Public anxiety about the dangers of railway travel was fed by the media coverage of lawsuits brought against train operators for failing to protect their passengers. In 1864, parliamentary legislation made British railway companies liable for the health and safety of their clients. It was from this juridical context that the earliest accounts of trauma emerged. Medico-legal professionals initially struggled to comprehend a category of injuries whose long-term consequences appeared as much psychological as physical. As the number of compensation claims rose, debates about the authenticity of the largely invisible psychical damage sustained in accidents focused on the phenomenon of 'railway spine', a condition first classified in Erichsen's pioneering lectures. In 1866, Erichsen published a paper entitled 'On Railway and Other Injuries of the Nervous System' in which he analysed the forms of nervous damage associated with spinal injuries from railway collisions. Throughout the 1870s, Erichsen's work gave rise to an increasing number of studies examining railway spine, most notably the research of Herbert Page. In 1883, Page published a paper on 'Injuries of the Spine and Spinal Cord without Apparent Mechanical Lesion', followed, in 1891, by his monograph *Railway Injuries: With Special Reference to Those of the Back and Nervous System*, in which he argued that the psychological effects of railway accidents such as fear and shock were *in and of themselves* capable of inducing enduring psychical damage, regardless of whether or not the patient had sustained a physical wound in the collision.

This revolutionary claim paved the way for subsequent conceptions of traumatic neuroses divorced from any physical injury. In so doing, the study of railway spine firmly linked the technological advancements of modernity to new and unprecedented forms of nervous disorder. The debates of this period prefigured and introduced many of the complexities that have since shadowed changing conceptualizations of trauma. As Luckhurst argues:

> Railway spine names a conjuncture of body and machine, the violent collision of technological modernity and human agency. This inaugural version of trauma is also intrinsically modern because it is, from the first, a *medico-legal* problem, which is to say that it is defined in and through the institutions and discourses marking the rise of the professional society in the nineteenth century. Rival experts would henceforth seek to define the protean signs of trauma in their specific disciplinary languages, partly recognizing that the very act of definition contributed to the mobility of symptoms.
>
> (2008: 24)

However, although it was certainly key to establishing the terms of early discourses surrounding trauma, the case of railway spine was not unique in revealing the complex relationship between the lived experience of modernity and the disparate forms of psychological injury to which modern subjects were exposed.

British debates over railway spine found a continental equivalent in controversies surrounding the establishment of the German welfare state. As in Britain, the mid-nineteenth century was a time of intense change in Germany, as an unprecedented population boom, the emergence of wage labour, the spread of unemployment and poverty, and the mass exodus of the rural working class to rapidly expanding cities transformed the social fabric. Conservatives perceived these developments as a threat to traditional German culture and values; wary that the growing social democratic movement would give rise to a revolutionary working-class politics, officials oversaw the creation of a prototypical welfare state designed to pacify workers while protecting the status quo. Organized around the administration of social insurance, this nascent welfare state had the dual benefit of reinforcing conventional patterns of power and governance while appearing to serve the interests of 'ordinary' citizens. As Greg Eghigian comments, 'insurance appeared to offer a particularly attractive way of fulfilling the professed aims of late nineteenth century social policy' (2001: 97), emphasizing 'the bourgeois and domestic virtues of order, thrift, prudence, far-sightedness, family life, frugality, orderliness, responsibility, contribution, labor, industriousness, and economy all at once' (2001: 98). The years 1840–1880 saw an enormous rise in the popularity of private life-insurance schemes, followed from 1883 to 1891 by the introduction of a compulsory national state-run general workers' insurance, 'deliberately placed in the industrial setting of capital-labor antagonism' in order to 'ensure social harmony and productivity' (2001: 99).

Over the course of the late nineteenth century, German medico-legal professionals developed a lexicon of trauma that facilitated the administration of compensation cases relating to industrial accidents. This emerging vocabulary resonated strongly with innovative discourses in clinical practice. As we have seen in the case of the UK, the mid-nineteenth century saw an explosion of interest in the mental sciences across Western Europe, which was manifested in Germany by a growing fascination with traumatic neurosis. Nowhere was this interest exemplified more clearly than in the work of Oppenheim. Like Erichsen before him, from 1883 to 1888 Oppenheim engaged in a study of principally male, working-class individuals who had been involved in railway and industrial accidents. In 1889, he published his findings in a monograph featuring the case histories of forty-one subjects. Oppenheim attributed traumatic neuroses to the presence of paralysing physical lesions in the brain and nervous system (as we will see, this theory was also expounded by Charcot in Paris, with whom Oppenheim corresponded closely). However, he argued that these physical injuries were only partially responsible for subsequent nervous disorders, suggesting that, in instances of traumatization resulting from industrial accidents, '[a]n important—and in many cases the major role—is played by the psyche: terror, emotional shock' (qtd in Lerner 2001: 178). This meant that even in cases where no visible physical injury was evident, it would be perfectly possible for the patient to suffer long-term psychological damage from the intense psychical shock of the accident.

Oppenheim's career was dogged by controversy. As his theory of trauma was 'swept up into large controversies about social insurance and its purportedly pathological effects' (Lerner 2001: 159), the physician was held personally responsible for 'a perceived epidemic of "pension neuroses"' (2001: 150). In the same year that Oppenheim published his monograph, Germany's Imperial Insurance Office recognized traumatic neurosis as a compensable injury in workplace lawsuits. However, as with lawsuits relating to railway spine in the UK, claimants often struggled to prove the authenticity of their claim to the satisfaction of insurers, who were predictably reluctant to acknowledge invisible injuries. The alleged suggestibility of the traumatized mind was exploitatively evoked by insurance companies to construct these cases as 'little more than a wave of mass malingering', 'intimately linked to what was believed to be a prevailing tendency among laborers to avoid work' (Eghigian 2001: 106).

Over the next three decades, arguments over claims relating to traumatic neuroses became increasingly litigious, as workers denied recompense took insurers to court to appeal their decisions. In turn, opponents of accident insurance law contended that the 1889 ruling risked actively *producing* traumatic neuroses by encouraging a pathological desire for pensions in a work-shy labour force. The effect, allegedly, was to sap the productivity of the German nation by rewarding laziness, generating, in the words of prominent psychiatrist Alfred Hoche, a 'people's epidemic' so grave that it constituted 'a cancer on the organism of [the] whole working class' (qtd in Lerner 2001: 150). From the 1890s onwards, the German medical community began to abandon Oppenheim's conception of traumatic neuroses in favour of a return to the older notion of hysteria, which will be discussed in more detail in the following section. This suited the economic interests of Germany's insurers and employers, for whom a diagnosis of hysteria was preferable to the label of traumatic neurosis. While traumatic neurosis was considered potentially incurable (opening the employer to indefinite pension payments), hysteria was understood as a temporary response to overwhelming stimuli, which might be overcome through treatment, facilitating the patient's return to work. The preference for hysteria over traumatic neurosis thus appeared financially, socially, and medically expedient, and the resulting backlash against Oppenheim was to have dramatic effects both for his professional reputation and for the way in which mental and nervous disorders were viewed and treated in Germany over the coming decades.

THE ORIGINS OF HYSTERIA

As the work of Erichsen and Oppenheim reveals, the late nineteenth century saw a paradigm shift in the mental sciences, which transformed medical attitudes towards nervous disorders. Instead of perceiving such diseases to be rooted in physiological causes, practitioners working within neuropathology, psychiatry, and the new discipline of psychoanalysis began to conceive of the existence of pathologies that might be purely or at least predominantly psychological in nature. While successive generations of mental health practitioners have revised and revisited this work, many of the foundational concepts that inform the study of trauma can be traced back to Charcot, Janet, and Freud. Although there are significant discrepancies in their accounts, these individuals remain highly influential in shaping the field of trauma studies into the twentieth and twenty-first centuries.

Charcot has been described as 'the foremost neurologist of late nineteenth century France' (Kushner 2009: 11). As one of his most prominent students, Joseph Babinski (whose work will be examined later in this chapter), remarked, 'to take away from neurology all the discoveries made by Charcot would be to render it unrecognizable' (qtd in Tan and Shigaki 2007: 383). Stationed at the Salpêtrière Hospital in Paris for thirty-three years, Charcot developed a groundbreaking system for the classification of nervous diseases. From 1878 to 1893, he embarked upon a detailed examination of traumatic neuroses to understand how and why relatively minor physical injuries could cause disabling psychical effects. While his findings would divide the fields of psychiatry and psychoanalysis, this project provided some of Charcot's most important legacies for the study of nervous disorders.

Although Charcot's research encompassed a wide range of illnesses, from multiple sclerosis to Parkinson's disease, it was his work on hysteria that proved most significant for the new disciplines of psychiatry and psychoanalysis. In line with the prevailing bias of French neurology in the nineteenth century, Charcot believed that hysterical symptoms emerged when an individual with a hereditary predisposition to nervous collapse was faced with an unexpected external shock. While defective tendencies could remain latent in the patient for decades, he argued, the triggering of hysterical symptoms (which might include amnesia, hallucinations, emotional disturbance, or delusions) was reliant on two causal factors: 'an unlocated physical functional lesion, the result of a physical trauma' and the 'psychological effects of fright and dissociation' (Fletcher 2013: 7).

Charcot's early investigations of hysteria were based on the study of female patients, whom he often put on display at his theatrical Tuesday lectures. In these lectures, he used live demonstrations to illustrate his clinical findings. Where previous generations of physicians had perceived hysterics, overwhelmingly identified as female, to be malingerers, Charcot contended that hysteria was a disease of the will that revealed unconscious thoughts and desires. He believed that such phenomena were best treated through a process of hypnotic suggestion, which would allow the patient to play out their fears and dreams in a 'safe' therapeutic environment. In his later practice, Charcot turned his attention to the victims of industrial and railway accidents. This move was revolutionary in terms of shifting established preconceptions about the identity of hysterics. While hysterics had previously been pictured in gendered and classed terms (as bored, affluent women), in focusing upon male, working-class patients injured in industrial accidents, Charcot's later work broadened the demographic of the condition, challenging engrained societal attitudes towards nervous disorders.

In studying his patients, Charcot came to believe that 'it is not the bodily blow per se that produced the disorder; rather, the mental experiencing of the traumatic episode, the emotional and ideational accompaniment of the event, carries the pathogenic charge and evokes symptoms' (Micale 2001: 122–23). In other words, traumatic symptoms were principally psychological, rather than physiological, in origin even if their onset was dependent upon the excitation of a pre-existing physical weakness. As influential as his work was in emphasizing the role of the unconscious in hysterical disorders, Charcot was never definitively able to identify the *cause* of hysteria, or to locate the mysterious lesion that, he believed, lay at the root of such pathologies. Accordingly, as Judith Herman notes, '[t]he ambition of Charcot's followers was to surpass his work by demonstrating the cause of hysteria. … In pursuit of their goal, these investigators found that it was not sufficient to observe and classify hysterics. It was necessary to talk with them'; this '[r]ivalry was particularly intense between Janet and Freud' (1992b: 11).

This brings us neatly to the work of Janet, another major figure in early psychiatry. Janet is described as both 'France's most important student of dissociation and hysteria' (van der Hart and Friedman 1989: 3) and 'the first psychologist to formulate a systematic therapeutic approach to post-traumatic psychopathology' (van der Hart *et al.* 1989: 379). In many ways, Janet's work on dissociation bridges the divide between Charcot's study of hysteria and Freud's work on trauma. A student of Charcot, who helped him establish his first psychiatric clinic at the Salpêtrière, Janet argued that *dissociation* was the underlying mechanism that connected hysteria and trauma. However, Janet's work became unfashionable after Charcot's death, and it was not until the late twentieth century that critics began to re-evaluate his legacy.

While the question of heredity remained an important element of Janet's work on hysteria, he was more convinced than Charcot that the causes of the disease were predominantly psychological. Janet's early psychiatric research revolved around the study of somnambulism. In contemporary terminology, the conditions that interested Janet might include anything from borderline personality disorder to multiple personality disorder and post-traumatic stress disorder; however, in the nineteenth century each of these neuroses was grouped under the heading of hysteria. Janet's research built upon a considerable body of earlier literature, which emerged out of the work of the 'magnetizers', who dedicated their careers to the investigation and performance of hypnosis in the late eighteenth and early nineteenth centuries, often with controversial results. As one of Janet's immediate predecessors, Hippolyte Taine, remarked, these practitioners were interested in the ways in which the same individual might experience 'two thoughts, two wills, two distinct actions, the one of which he is aware, the other of which he is not aware and which he ascribes to invisible beings' (qtd in van der Hart and Horst 1989: 2). Janet regarded this experience of multiple fields of consciousness as a form of dissociation through which the conscious mind might be split into two or more systems or subsystems of varying degrees of complexity. Most often, though not exclusively, triggered by a traumatic event, dissociation results in the production of hysterical symptoms, including sleepwalking, hallucinations, nightmares, and forms of automatic writing, through which the dissociated subject struggles to rid themselves of a fixed idea (an *idée fixe*) by which they have become possessed.

As Janet elaborated in his major publications (1894; 1895), *idées fixes* are the products of traumatic memories: 'thoughts or mental images which assume exaggerated proportions, have a high emotional charge and, in hysterical patients, are isolated from the habitual personality (or personal consciousness)' (van der Hart and Horst 1989: 7). Distinguishing between feelings, which form part of the healthy regulating system of 'normal' consciousness, and emotions, over which the subject has little or no conscious control, Janet argued that extreme emotions, triggered by an overwhelming event, exert 'a disintegrative effect on the mind' (van der Hart and Horst 1989: 7). Split from personal consciousness, traumatic memories 'persist as fixed ideas, which may develop subconsciously. They manifest themselves at times in dreams, flashbacks, and other dissociative episodes' (1989: 7). Anticipating Freud's later work on the associative nature of trauma, Janet categorized two distinct forms of *idées fixes*: first, dreams and memories directly associated with the traumatizing event that infiltrate personal consciousness and disrupt it; second, fragments or feelings that are tangentially linked to the event but not explicitly related to it, such as inexplicable phobias, repeated nightmares, fantasies, or hallucinations.

Over a career that spanned nearly sixty years, Janet's research was dedicated to exploring how traumatic events may trigger dissociative processes that split consciousness and result in the production of hysterical symptoms. A strong proponent of hypnosis, Janet believed that, by inducing a form of artificial somnambulism in the patient, it is possible to engage the memories, thoughts, and personalities that reside in the split parts of consciousness. This method was founded on the assumption that patients suffering from a dissociative disorder are highly suggestible, hence the widespread use of hypnosis as a primary means of treating hysteria. Contending that dissociated subjects experience a narrowed field of consciousness (restricted in order to repress the existence of undesirable memories or fantasies), Janet believed that the process of suggestion provides a way of addressing the subconscious, with the aim of reintegrating the divided mind. As Luckhurst notes, in direct contrast to current norms of psychiatric practice,

> Trauma was not to be recovered, affirmed, respected, abreacted, mourned, assimilated, brought to closure—the familiar language and trajectory of contemporary psychotherapy. Instead, a traumatic memory was to be manipulated, recomposed, or replaced with another sometimes falsified memory or else entirely erased.
>
> (2008: 44)

Janet's dogged adherence to the process of hypnosis was a major factor in the marginalization of his legacy, and it was this controversial method of falsifying or erasing traumatic memories that led Freud to break with the practice of hypnotic suggestion. Today, it is Freud's work that casts the longer shadow over the fields of psychoanalysis and trauma studies; however, as with most aspects of his career, this legacy is controversial. Critics have vigorously debated the role that Freud has played in shaping current conceptions of trauma, some wishing to uphold his primacy and others seeking to decentralize his contribution. Certainly, it is difficult to attribute a fixed conception of trauma to Freud. While his early psychiatric practice was strongly informed by Charcot's investigations into hysteria, from the 1890s Freud's research acquired its own direction, moving away from the field of psychiatry towards the new discipline of psychoanalysis. Freud's thought continued to evolve in contradictory ways over the next four decades. Uncertain how to handle this inconsistent legacy, scholars have privileged different texts in their reflections on Freud's work. Nonetheless, most cite *Studies on Hysteria* (Freud and Breuer 1895) and *Beyond the Pleasure Principle*

(1920; see Freud 2010a) as key interventions in the literature on trauma, with some, notably Cathy Caruth and Luckhurst, also positioning *Moses and Monotheism* (1939; see Freud 2010b) as a significant milestone in Freud's thought.

From October 1885 to February 1886, Freud studied with Charcot at the Salpêtrière (he later translated Charcot's notes on traumatic hysteria). Given his proximity to such a seminal figure, it is unsurprising that Freud's 1893 publication 'On the Psychical Mechanism of Hysterical Phenomena', co-written with Josef Breuer, followed very much in the vein of both Charcot's study of hysteria and Janet's writing on dissociation. In this text, Freud and Breuer conceptualized traumatic hysteria as a disorder of memory that persists below the threshold of consciousness. Like their predecessors, at this stage Freud and Breuer believed that hysterics register traumatic memory in displaced forms, which could be brought to the surface via a treatment of hypnosis. Crucially, however, as John Fletcher notes, it is also in this text that Freud's understanding of trauma first 'exits from the terrain of neurology entirely in order to formulate precisely what Freud calls the *psychical* mechanism for the production of hysterical symptoms', rendering the work 'the urtext of psychoanalysis' (2013: 23). Over the course of the next decade, Freud would continue to rework Charcot's physiological account of hysteria into a psychoanalytic theory of trauma. As Micale observes, for Freud, 'Charcot's cases opened the way toward the possibility of a … general psychological theory of the neuroses' (2001: 129), which 'elevated the medical idea of trauma from secondary to primary etiological status. [Freud and Breuer] then linked trauma to the notions of psychosexual motivation and unconscious repression and pushed it deep into the emotional past of the individual' (2001: 128–29), reversing Charcot's hierarchy of trauma and hysteria to position the latter as a mere symptom of the former.

The next significant leap in Freud's thought came in *Studies on Hysteria* (1895), also written with Breuer, which focused primarily on the relationship between trauma and sexuality. It is here that Freud's model of trauma began to gain in complexity, introducing a number of important concepts that would define his later work.

Tracing traumatic hysteria to the belated return of sexual experiences that had been repressed in childhood, *Studies on Hysteria* was Freud's first attempt to conceive of trauma as a layered pathology related to forgotten libidinal neuroses. While Janet positioned the subconscious as the product of traumatic experience in those unable to assimilate dissociated parts of their memory, Freud regarded it as an integral element of the mind. Instead of drawing a direct cause-and-effect relationship between a discrete catalysing event (such as a railway or industrial accident) and subsequent psychological disturbances, Freud and Breuer came to regard the origins of trauma as embedded in a *series* of occurrences that act as triggers for earlier memories. This implied that traumatic symptoms mark the *belated* psychical registration of a past experience (such as an early sexual encounter) that did not necessarily appear significant until it was unexpectedly recalled by a later event. Thus, as Ruth Leys contends,

> Freud problematized the originary status of the traumatic event by arguing that it was not the experience itself which acted traumatically, but its delayed retrieval as a *memory* after the individual had entered sexual maturity and could grasp its sexual meaning.
>
> (2000: 20)

After *Studies on Hysteria,* Freud began to flesh out the relationship between traumatic neuroses and sexual development. Alarmed by the potential implications of his seduction theory, which, taken to its logical conclusion, would point to the endemic nature of what today we might recognize as infantile sexual abuse, Freud moved away from understanding trauma as a belated response to an early sexual experience towards a prototype of the Oedipus complex. This model positioned repressed sexual desires as a universal aspect of infantile development, meaning that traumatic symptoms could belatedly emerge from the reactivation of latent *fantasies* rather than buried sexual *experiences.* This move marked the final transition from a physiological model of trauma, which saw mental neuroses as a psychological response to an external shock, to a theory of psychoanalysis, which posited the existence of repressed memories as fundamental to the structure of consciousness. While his understanding of trauma continued to oscillate throughout the late nineteenth century, this period would cement Freud's break from the earlier work of Charcot and Janet, as well as the end of his collaboration with Breuer.

Freud's research on trauma thus shaped the model of consciousness that would later constitute the core of his psychoanalytic work. However, the onset of the First World War called Freud's libidinal theory of trauma into question, as large numbers of soldiers returned from conflict with symptoms of trauma that were more easily, and immediately, attributable to the overwhelming experience of mechanized warfare than to the manifestation of repressed sexual urges. While Freud did not entirely relinquish his libidinal model of traumatic neurosis, he became increasingly aware of the need to account for the psychical impact of wartime experiences. This realization caused a third shift in his understanding of trauma, which can be most clearly seen in *Beyond the Pleasure Principle*, published in 1920. In this text, Freud positioned the death drive as the psychic exception to the otherwise dominant pleasure principle, which he defined as the organizing structure of normal psychological life. According to Freud, the pleasure principle resembles a regulatory mechanism, which 'endeavours to keep the quantity of [psychical] excitement … as low as possible, or at least to keep it constant' (2010a: 4–5). Under normal circumstances, the ego is prevented from being overwhelmed by stimuli from the external world by a protective shield, which enables the subject to absorb (or 'bind') their experiences into a coherent whole. However, in exceptional conditions, 'excitations from outside powerful enough to break through the protective shield' (2010a: 45) take the subject unawares, causing 'a breach in an otherwise efficacious barrier against stimuli'. With 'the pleasure principle … put out of action', there is 'no longer any possibility of preventing the mental apparatus from being flooded with large amounts of stimulus' (2010a: 46). Following this model, the widespread traumatization of soldiers in the First World War could be explained by the fact that, overwhelmed by the unprecedented violence of mechanized warfare, they were left without the psychical defences needed to protect them from the horrors of the battlefield.

In the aftermath of the First World War, Freud's focus on trauma began to shift towards an acknowledgement of the ways in which specific historical circumstances disrupt the normative functioning of consciousness. However, as Leys notes, his 'writings of the 1920s and 1930s remained fraught with doubt and vacillation' (2000: 24). It is not until his final departure on the subject, in *Moses and Monotheism* (published posthumously in 1939, the year of his death), that Freud was to fully assign a broader historical dimension to his theory of trauma. As Caruth contends, *Moses and Monotheism* represents Freud's attempt to connect the individual experience of trauma to 'the collective, transgenerational, and religious history' (1996: 67) of the Jewish people. Here, Freud argues that Jewish history can be best explained by a traumatic rupture in its monotheistic tradition, which arises from the failure to fully or, at least, punctually claim the murder of Moses as part of Semitic heritage. For Freud, the repression of Moses's murder led to a crisis of identity, as a result of which the Jews were unable to recognize themselves as God's chosen people. Here, Freud draws a direct correspondence between 'the problem of traumatic neuroses and that of Jewish Monotheism' (2010b: 109), suggesting that both are strongly defined by 'the feature which one might term *latency*' (2010b: 110). While this connection may seem tangential, to say the least, in making this claim, Freud is working on the assumption that, just as the traumatized subject will undergo a period of belatedness before memories of the originary event are able to surface, so 'in the history of the Jewish religion there is a long period—after the breaking away from the Moses religion—during which no trace is to be found of the monotheistic idea'. This raises 'the possibility that the solution of [the] problem [of reconciling Jewish historical identity with itself] is to be sought in a special psychological situation' (2010b: 110).

In addition to marking the finale to Freud's career-long study of neuroses, *Moses and Monotheism* demonstrates most clearly how changing understandings of trauma are imbricated with the wider historical conditions from which they emerge. In a letter written to Arnold Zweig in 1933, Freud offers some crucial reflections on the ways in which the anti-Semitism of the Nazi regime in Germany had informed the direction of his own work, remarking that, '[f]aced with the new persecutions, one asks oneself again how the Jews have come to be what they are and why they have attracted this undying hatred' (qtd in Caruth 1996: 12). As we shall see in the following section, clinical approaches to the diagnosis and treatment of trauma have been recurrently shaped by the spectre of violence, pre-emptive and retrospective. Indeed, over the course of the twentieth century, the connection between trauma and war became ever more intimate.

INVISIBLE WOUNDS OF WAR

Micale and Lerner note that '[t]he nexus of trauma, psychiatry, and modernity ... is nowhere dramatized more sharply than in the First World War' (2001: 16). Across the United States and Europe, the prevalence of traumatized soldiers did much to expose and challenge existing attitudes towards nervous disorders. However, the differential diagnosis and treatment of veterans reflected, in turn, the various modes of 'scientific nationalisms' (2001: 15) at work in these contexts. The diversity of responses to the trauma of war was reflected in the breadth of terminology used to account for the various neuroses associated with the experience of conflict. As Micale and Lerner comment, '[a] varied and colorful nomenclature emerged—shellshock, war strain, gas neurosis, buried alive neurosis, soldier's heart, war neurasthenia, anxiety neurosis' (2001: 17). These semantic differences should not be seen as mere idiosyncrasies but as a direct result of the national and institutional politics that informed the treatment of mental illness. As Bruna Bianchi asserts,

> In each of the belligerent countries of the Great War, military trauma, emotional suffering, and daily exposure to violence and death caused mental distress beyond all expectations. Psychiatrists in each country were called on to observe, select, and cure, and were forced to examine their views of mental illness in light of the war experiences.
> (2001: 222)

In Germany, the advent of the First World War marked the end of Oppenheim's career. In December 1914, Oppenheim was made responsible for the treatment of nervous disorders in soldiers at a military hospital in Berlin. After extensive study of his patients, Oppenheim contended that the symptoms of 'war neurosis' corresponded with the forms of 'traumatic neurosis' he had identified more than two decades earlier. However, as Lerner remarks, 'many German doctors feared that the war—and particularly the revival of Oppenheim's ideas—would serve as an excuse for a massively debilitating epidemic among soldiers and veterans, a war-time parallel to the so-called pension neuroses among "work-shy" laborers' (2001: 156). Faced with undeniable evidence of pervasive nervous disorders resulting from exposure to mechanized warfare, German doctors 'had two diagnostic choices for war neuroses: They could diagnose traumatic neurosis, guaranteeing their patients indefinite pension payments, or they could choose hysteria, which, attributing symptoms to abnormal psychological reactions, made rehabilitation and an end to pensioning seem possible' (2001: 157). Anxious to avoid both the potentially enormous economic cost to the state and the possible disruption to the war effort that might arise from widespread discharge of soldiers suffering from traumatic neuroses, Oppenheim's colleagues opted overwhelmingly for the latter option in a move that echoed the debates over industrial accidents some decades before. Accordingly, as Lerner asserts, the 'enduring fear of epidemic pension hysteria haunted Oppenheim and contributed to the vehement rejection of his theories. Convinced that Germany's economic and military strength hung in the balance, his opponents approached the debate as a patriotic battle' (2001: 171).

In Germany, the diagnostic privileging of hysteria over war neurosis was reflective of the desire to reduce the availability of pension claims for soldiers traumatized by their combat experience. In Italy, meanwhile, the military mobilized the language of hysteria to accuse soldiers suffering from nervous disorders of malingering or hereditary weakness. Over the course of the First World War, the work of the French neurologist Joseph Babinski was appropriated to serve the ends of the Italian military, which attempted to turn public opinion against traumatized (or, in the preferred terminology of the time, hysterical) soldiers by discrediting their claims to psychological injury. Like many of the leading psychiatrists of the nineteenth century, Babinski had studied under Charcot. However, following the death of his former teacher, Babinski sought to 'dismember' Charcot's legacy by rejecting his theory of hysteria. Babinski repositioned hysteria as 'a disease of false symptoms', on the basis that the absence of a physical wound meant that, theoretically at least, nothing stood in the way of its '"correction", except the will of the patient' (Roudebush 2001: 261). While this theory found only limited support in the psychiatric community during the first years of the twentieth century, from 1914 onwards, 'the pressures of war and the need for a simple and patriotic definition of hysteria [brought] Babinski's approach decisively into favor' (2001: 261), both in his home nation of France and, even more conclusively, in Italy, where national engagement in the war had been shadowed by controversy and dispute.

The unpopularity of the conflict among the civilian population was reinforced by a long-standing cultural antipathy towards the Italian military. The military hierarchy was remarkably unsympathetic to the challenges faced by their new recruits, and, as Bianchi notes, 'lack of discipline, desertion, and rebellion were widely interpreted as psychic unfitness for communal life; as signs of immature development; or as defects of character and morals' (2001: 224). Such attitudes were strongly informed by elitist ideas, which regarded working-class soldiers as prone to degenerative hereditary conditions such as hysteria. These conceptions resonated with the earlier work of Babinski in a number of ways. Because Babinski, like the Italian military establishment, regarded hysteria as a failure of willpower, he believed that its symptoms could be cured through a process of persuasion, which involved convincing the patient of the folly of their delusions. For the Italian military, the notion that 'the treatment of hysteria consisted of countering bad influences (suggestions) with good ones (persuasion) lent itself to the construction of a variety of therapeutic scenarios' (Roudebush 2001: 262), alternately aimed at rehabilitating soldiers and returning them to conflict, or weeding out potentially destabilizing elements and removing them from combat. Mobilized for allegedly patriotic ends, Babinski's earlier work on hysteria gave officers and officials a way of combating dissension by dismissing nervous disorders as failures of the will and forcibly 'persuading' soldiers to execute their duties, or blaming military failures on working-class factions that had been rendered 'degenerate' by hereditary conditioning.

While the treatment of traumatized veterans proved particularly contentious for the defeated nations, Italy and Germany were not the only countries that struggled with the question of how to cope with psychologically damaged soldiers during and after the First World War. The French government mobilized a diagnosis of 'war hysteria' to absolve itself of responsibility for the psychical legacies of the war, arguing that any long-term psychological damage was caused by the mental weakness of individual soldiers rather than the conditions to which the state had exposed them. Although returning troops were generally treated more sympathetically in the UK and the US, the issue of shell-shock proved no less politicized in these allied nations than for the central powers. Indeed, the Anglo-American contexts demonstrate most clearly how the legacies of the First World War transformed established attitudes to mental illness, revealing the crucial and long-lasting role the conflict has played in changing clinical attitudes to trauma.

The UK government displayed a certain ambivalence to traumatized veterans, exemplified by the publication of the *Report of the War Office Committee of Enquiry into 'Shell-Shock'* in 1922. As Ted Bogacz notes, 'the questions posed by the shell-shock crisis … ultimately threatened a number of traditional moral values' (1989: 227), raising questions 'not only about the origins and treatment of mental illness but also whether formerly firm lines of moral behavior could continue to be maintained in light of this new knowledge' (1989: 236). Perceived as 'a legal, medical and moral half-way house in a society used to a clear division between the mad and the sane' (1989: 229), the conundrum of shell-shock threatened to overturn accepted norms of practice for a medical profession still largely wedded to the notion that mental illness chiefly arose from a physiological defect, such as the elusive lesion to which Charcot had gestured some decades earlier. However, the findings of the committee were significant for the ways in which they revised many of the conceptual and disciplinary tensions that informed the study of trauma throughout the late nineteenth and early twentieth centuries, and pre-empted a number of the complexities that would later affect the field of trauma studies into the twentieth and twenty-first centuries: highlighting the disjunctions between physiological and psychical accounts of traumatic causality, revealing the disciplinary fractures between psychiatric and psychoanalytic modes of diagnosis and treatment, raising questions about the verifiability of traumatic neuroses, demonstrating how trauma breaches the boundaries between public and private life, and foregrounding the imbrication between medico-legal regimes of knowledge and the agendas of the public-political sphere.

The aftermath of the war was even more revolutionary in transforming the understanding of mental illness in the American context. As Caroline Cox notes, '[i]n the United States, as in Britain, the military establishment saw a blurred line between shellshock and cowardice' (2001: 291). However, the postwar lobbying of the American Legion, a veterans organization founded in 1919, sought to transform the public image of traumatized soldiers by portraying veterans as 'ordinary men who had done their patriotic duty and suffered as a result' (2001: 291). In changing shell-shock from a mark of cowardice to a badge of heroism, the legion engendered a cultural and institutional shift in attitudes towards mental illness. The establishment of the Veterans Bureau (later the Veterans Administration) in 1921 led to the creation of an infrastructure of psychiatric clinics and hospitals for soldiers suffering from shell-shock. With a larger budget than any other department (one-fifth of the federal funds), the bureau turned the US government into a significant provider of mental health care. These successes were compounded by congressional approval of the Reed–Johnson bill in 1924, which recognized nervous disorders as war-related conditions that qualified for treatment and compensation (Cox 2001: 299).

From Freud's reflections in *Beyond the Pleasure Principle* to the establishment of the Veterans Bureau, the aftermath of the First World War offers a clear illustration of how psychiatric attitudes to trauma are transformed by historical circumstances. These precedents established an intimate relationship between trauma and warfare, which was reinforced by the catastrophic events of the mid-twentieth century. In 1941, just prior to the United States' entry into the Second World War, a monograph entitled *The Traumatic Neuroses of War* was published by Abram Kardiner, a psychiatrist who had been psychoanalysed by Freud in the 1920s and who had worked in the United States Veterans Hospital from 1922 to 1925. Kardiner's work marked the first of a series of prominent publications that firmly inscribed the connection between trauma and warfare. In 1945, Roy Grinker and John Spiegel published *War Neuroses*, a reflection on the experiences of American psychiatric casualties in the Second World War, and in 1955, the Veterans Administration published a follow-up study of soldiers diagnosed with war neuroses. However, while all of these accounts reinscribed the connection between combat and trauma, each contained significant discrepancies and omissions, which made it difficult to assemble anything like coherent diagnostic criteria. It was not until after the Vietnam War that 'a diagnostic metalanguage' (Young 1995: 94) for the treatment of trauma—or post-traumatic stress disorder (PTSD), as it came to be known—was developed.

AN INTEGRATED APPROACH

As Allan Young notes, '[t]he origins of the PTSD diagnosis are inextricably connected with the lives of American veterans of the Vietnam War, with their experiences as combatants, and later as patients of the Veterans Administration (VA) Medical System' (1995: 108). Robert Jay Lifton's intensive study of the psychological effects of the Vietnam War on American veterans is particularly illustrative in underscoring this symbiosis. In *Home from the War* (1973), Lifton builds upon his earlier research with Hiroshima survivors at the end of the Second World War (1967) and his clinical work as an American Air Force psychiatrist in Korea. An active anti-war protestor who, along with fellow psychiatrist Chaim Shatan, worked closely with the radical veterans group Veterans against the War, Lifton 'spoke to about four hundred veterans, spent more than one hundred and fifty hours in rap groups ..., and eighty hours in individual interviews' (1973: 18). He also testified before the US Senate's Cranston Subcommittee on the psychological effects of Vietnam and conducted 'a series of intensive interviews ... with a GI who had been at My Lai' (1973: 17), the Vietnamese village where American troops massacred more than 500 people, including women and children, in 1968. Lifton's study adopts a 'psychohistorical' approach to the trauma of Vietnam, drawing 'a dialectic between the specificity of the Vietnam War and its relationship to all war' (1973: 19). He notes the similarities between the psychological legacies of Vietnam and those of other wars (the Thirty Years' War, the Napoleonic Wars, the Crimean War, and the First and Second World Wars, among others), but insists that '[t]here is something special about Vietnam veterans. Everyone who has contact with them seems to agree that they are different from veterans of other wars. A favorite word to describe them is "alienated"' (1973: 35).

For many veterans, the traumatic combat conditions to which they were exposed in Vietnam were compounded by their return to an ambivalent, and at times hostile, homeland. The majority of veterans returned to the United States between 1964 and 1975 after serving a tour of around twelve months. Support for veterans with ongoing psychological difficulties was severely limited, and they were frequently left to devise their own coping mechanisms to deal with what they had seen and done, which often meant self-medicating. The high levels of suicides, anti-social behaviour, alcoholism, and drug abuse among returning veterans ensured that '[t]he "crazy" Vietnam vet—angry, violent, and emotionally unstable—had become an American archetype' (Young 1995: 108) before the war had even come to an end. Lifton suggests that, as a result of their experiences in Vietnam, veterans felt betrayed by the government and evidenced 'greater distrust of institutions and unwillingness to be awed by traditional authorities' (1973: 35) than veterans of previous wars. This mistrust, he continues, extended to psychiatric professionals employed by the armed forces and, in particular, to the very same Veterans Administration that had been established in the wake of the First World War to champion the psychiatric needs of returning soldiers.

Lifton indicts military clinicians for their complicity in the war effort, charging them with practising 'the psychiatry of the executioner', helping 'men adjust to their own atrocities' 'in collusion with the military in conveying to individual GIs an overall organizational message: "Do your indiscriminate killing with confidence that you will receive expert medical-psychological help if needed"' (1973: 414). The help that *was* offered to soldiers was often inadequate, aimed at facilitating their quick return to combat rather than their long-term mental well-being. Accordingly, Lifton argues,

> there is evidence ... that large numbers of [veterans] feel themselves to be 'hurting' and in need of psychological help but avoid contact with the Veterans Administration. They associate it with the war-military-government establishment, with the forces responsible for a hated ordeal, or with their suspicion (whether on the basis of hearsay or personal experience) that VA doctors are likely to interpret their rage at everything connected with the war as no more than their own individual problems.
>
> (1973: 35)

Faced with this situation, Lifton identifies a general crisis in psychiatry, exploring 'its corruptions as revealed in the Vietnam War' and arguing that it requires 'a transformation of its own' (1973: 20). Over the course of the 1970s, along with a loose network of veterans associations and psychiatrists, Lifton would dedicate his work to bringing about this transformation.

In 1972, Shatan published an opinion article in the *New York Times* in which he outlined a condition he described as 'post-Vietnam disorder', a specific response to 'delayed massive trauma' (1972), which saw veterans suffering from feelings of rage, isolation, and numbing. Two years later, the American Psychiatric Association's (APA) Council on Research and Development assembled a Task Force on Nomenclature to compile the third edition of the *Diagnostic and Statistical Manual of Mental Disorders* (DSM-III). The editor of DSM-III was Robert Spitzer, a professor of psychiatry at Columbia University. In 1975, Spitzer was approached by Lifton and Shatan, who requested that he form a subcommittee to consider including post-Vietnam syndrome in the manual. While Spitzer was initially wary, he subsequently gave Lifton and Shatan permission to form a working group on the renamed 'post-combat disorder'. In January 1978, the group presented its final report to the Committee on Reactive Disorders, which recommended that 'catastrophic stress disorder', ultimately re-termed 'post-traumatic stress disorder', be added to DSM-III in the section on anxiety disorders (Young 1995: 109–11).

This insertion was far from plain sailing. The working group's proposal met with opposition from the VA, Veterans Service

Organizations (for soldiers who had fought in conflicts prior to Vietnam), and the House and Senate Veterans Affairs Committees. The VA's reluctance to acknowledge the ongoing psychiatric issues experienced by veterans can be attributed in part to an anxiety about its own complicity in encouraging traumatized soldiers to return to conflict and its failure to adequately treat traumatized veterans on their return to the United States. Veterans Service Organizations, meanwhile, were wary of the claims made by Shatan, Lifton, and others, believing that

> proponents [of the PTSD diagnosis] were part of the most visible and activist symbol of the anti-war movement in the United States: Vietnam Veterans Against the War, who were 'probably all crazy before they got into the service in the first place'.
>
> (Fuller 1985: 6)

The House and Senate Veterans Affairs Committees had more immediate financial concerns, as Young notes:

> It was clear to everyone that the proposed diagnosis would have important fiscal and manpower implications for the VA. It would make the VA the primary care provider for all present and future cases of PTSD affecting veterans ... The federal government and its designated agent, the VA, could anticipate substantial compensation claims from large numbers of veterans ... Further, VA regulations would permit veterans with PTSD to seek retroactive compensation, going back to the time of their initial psychiatric (mis)diagnoses. These changes would require additional funds from Congress.
>
> (1995: 113)

Conversely, this growing opposition to the proposed addition to DSM-III had the effect of galvanizing support for the inclusion of PTSD within the APA. With the APA's experts behind PTSD, the government had little choice but to follow suit. In 1979, the Senate Veterans Affairs Committee authorized the VA to recognize PTSD among Vietnam veterans. The following year the VA accepted PTSD as a compensable disorder, and DSM-III was finally published in 1980.

The first version of DSM-III established the following diagnostic criteria for PTSD:

- PTSD is a reaction to a catalysing event that is 'outside the range of usual human experience'; 'a recognizable stressor that would evoke significant symptoms of distress in almost anyone'.
- The traumatizing event is re-experienced in a number of different ways: 'recurrent, intrusive, and distressful recollections of the event'; 'dreams of the event'; 'sudden acting or feeling as if the traumatic events were recurring, because of an association with an environmental or ideational stimulus'.
- PTSD patients experience 'a numbing of response to the external world' along with other observable symptoms, including 'hyperalertness', 'sleep disturbance', 'guilt about surviving', 'memory impairment', and 'avoidance of activities that arouse the recollection of the traumatic event'.

(American Psychiatric Association 1980: 236–38)

The APA's definition marked a seminal moment in the history of trauma because it gave trauma official disease status for the first time. It also represented the first unified theory of trauma—earlier research had always been limited to particular groups of people in particular situations (victims of railway or industrial accidents, hysterical women, combat veterans, rape and incest victims). In consequence, PTSD was rapidly institutionalized and quickly became the predominant model for diagnosing traumatic disorders. However, critics have subsequently suggested that there are significant blind-spots in the APA's categorization of PTSD. Their critiques have focused on four major concerns (the third and fourth of which are explored in more detail in Chapter 4): first, that the APA's definition of PTSD is disciplinarily biased, marginalizing psychodynamic perspectives on trauma; second, that the diagnosis of PTSD, and the central role placed upon healing in the treatment programme, could be used to 'medicalize' survivors, thereby denying them political agency; third, that its specific list of diagnostic criteria unduly restricts the kinds of experiences that can be recognized as traumatic; and fourth, that the concept of PTSD legitimates the suffering of certain subject groups above others, producing an implicitly Western-centric model of trauma that marginalizes the suffering of non-white individuals and communities.

After 1980, the criteria laid out in DSM-III were quickly naturalized as the de facto diagnostic model for PTSD. As Young observes, '[o]nce DSM-III had been adopted by the APA, researchers and clinicians found good reasons to adopt its conception of mental disorders', whereas 'researchers and clinicians who resisted these conventions could count on being excluded from these areas and their resources' (1995: 102). While the APA's introduction to DSM-III celebrates the manual's ability to provide 'a way of talking about mental disorders that is not particular to any theoretical orientation' (Young 1995: 94), the final text does not necessarily reflect its alleged disciplinary neutrality. The structure of DSM-III was determined by Spitzer and a small team of psychiatrists, all of whom identified with the rigorously empirical work of the German clinician Emil Kraepelin, which positioned psychiatric disorders as akin to physical ailments, with a discrete and observable causality and externally visible symptoms. This approach is very different from the psychodynamic perspective adopted by Freud and his followers, all of whom chart a more complex and associative model of traumatic etiology. It is thus unsurprising that DSM-III has been accused of ignoring 'the "theoretical diversity" of American psychiatry' (Young 1995: 104).

Such concerns point to a reification of psychiatric work on PTSD that is at odds with the progressive widening of the parameters of cultural trauma theory explored in Chapter 3. Alongside the naturalization of certain disciplinary perspectives, the explanation for this lies in part in the role played by the VA in funding PTSD research. As Young comments,

> two decades after the fall of Saigon, scientific research on PTSD continues to be based largely on veterans of the Vietnam War. And the Veterans Administration remains the most significant source of research funds and cases (diagnosed veterans) for studying the disorder.
>
> (1995: 111)

Having grudgingly accepted PTSD as a compensable disorder in 1980, the VA was keen to promote a very specific model of treatment and recovery. Kalí Tal argues that this approach, which secured the backing of the Veterans Affairs Committees in the House of Representatives and the Senate in 1985, created a process of 'medicalization' through which veterans were perceived to 'suffer from an "illness" that can be "cured" within existing or slightly modified structures of institutionalized medicine and psychiatry' (1996: 6). Tal suggests that this process disenfranchises veterans, rebranding their horrific memories as products of a 'sick' mind and denying them political agency. As she explains:

> Though we may be confounded by angry activist Vietnam vets marching in the streets and hurling their medals back at the government that awarded them, we are quite clear on what to do with 'patients'—we place them under the care of experts and we 'treat' them with therapy or drugs. We continue the therapy until they are healed.
>
> (1996: 145)

Following the same logic deployed by insurers in industrializing Germany and the Italian military during the First World War, this approach implies that the trauma of Vietnam was caused by the soldiers' own psychological weaknesses rather than by the impossible situation in which they were placed by their own government. By claiming that the trauma of Vietnam could be 'cured' with relevant medical intervention, the VA also served to downplay the psychological legacy of conflict and minimize the US government's long-term responsibility to its veterans.

Thus, the discourse of trauma became no less politicized after its official recognition—far from it. During the 1970s and 1980s, feminist activists argued that the intimate association between PTSD and the public violence of warfare would have the effect of excluding 'private' scenes of conflict, such as domestic abuse, from the field of traumatic experience. As Judith Herman argues, '[n]ot until the women's liberation movement of the 1970s was it recognized that the most common post-traumatic disorders are not those of men in war but of women in civilian life' (1992b: 28). While rape was recognized as a potential catalyst for PTSD in the original diagnostic criteria of DSM-III, other forms of domestic violence were not, leading feminist organizations and psychiatric professionals to stage a series of consciousness-raising events aimed at challenging the impression that PTSD was necessarily linked to a discrete catalysing event 'outside the range of usual human experience', such as war or rape. These groups argued for greater public recognition of domestic violence, like spousal abuse, that was routine, everyday, and sustained. Herman was one of the first female psychiatrists to work with the APA in preparation for the second, revised version of DSM-III (1987). In 'opening up the process of writing the diagnostic canon, which had been the preserve of a small group of men' (Herman 1992b: 117), these women sought to pioneer a more complicated model of trauma that would allow for a diverse range of symptoms and causes. As Herman comments, 'post-traumatic stress disorder fails to capture either the protean symptomatic manifestations of prolonged, repeated trauma or the profound deformations of personality that occur in captivity'. By contrast, 'complex post-traumatic stress disorder' understands responses to trauma as 'a spectrum of conditions rather than as a single disorder', ranging 'from a brief stress reaction that gets better by itself and never qualifies for a diagnosis, to classic or simple post-traumatic stress disorder, to the complex syndrome of prolonged, repeated trauma' (1992b: 119).

Herman's notion of a 'complex' model of trauma was vitally important in legitimating the traumatic, and often silent, experience of millions of women in the United States and beyond. However, as recent interventions have argued, despite its undoubted significance, Herman's work perpetuates certain elisions in the psychiatric literature on PTSD. As Claire Stocks contends, Herman's model of subjectivity remains reliant on 'specifically Western conceptions of the self' (2007: 73), which understand identity as essentially coherent and stable. Laura Brown expands:

> Trauma does not happen to a generic human being any more than it is generic itself, and the ways in which humans translate their inner biological states of posttraumatic disequilibrium into outward expression of distress are strongly affected by culture and context.
>
> (2008: 7)

In taking this into account, Brown argues, diagnostic models of trauma need to acknowledge the systemic and everyday experience of sexism, racism, classism, and homophobia, among other forms of discrimination, *alongside* additional stressors such as '[d]isability, immigration status, experiences of colonization, and other social locations [that] have informed people's experiences of identity, and thus of trauma', but 'largely gone unaddressed within the mental health discourse' (2008: 10). The Western-centric nature of clinical and cultural theories of trauma will be analysed further in Chapter 4. For the moment, it is worth noting that, despite the clear relationship between the publication of DSM-III and the Vietnam War, the APA's manual promotes a peculiarly timeless and a-cultural model of PTSD, which belies its connection to the particular context of its origins. While the DSM has been revised repeatedly since 1980, this early inattention to historical and cultural specificity produced a homogenizing model of trauma that has since lent itself to overexpansion and overgeneralization.

THE AGE OF TRAUMA

Luckhurst describes trauma as a 'cusp term' (2008: 209): 'a conceptual knot whose successful permeation must be understood by the impressive range of elements it ties together and which allows it to travel to such diverse places in the network of knowledge' (2008: 14) as 'psychology, medicine, law, military history, literature, autobiography, confessional TV, fine art and film' (2008: 209). This chapter has illustrated how, since its emergence in the late nineteenth century, trauma has insistently moved beyond the psychiatric realm to infiltrate multiple areas of the public sphere: the disputes over railway spine and industrial accidents in the nineteenth century concerned lawyers and insurers; First World War debates surrounding shell-shock implicated governments and the armed forces; and the discussions surrounding the APA's categorization of PTSD in the 1970s involved veterans groups, anti-war protestors, and feminist activists. Luckhurst argues that this process of 'transvaluation' reached its zenith in the early 1990s, when the concept of trauma began in earnest to 'escape narrow professional discourses and diffuse into the wider culture' (2008: 76). So widespread was the resulting 'traumatophilia' (2008: 39) that 'a new kind of articulation of subjectivity emerged … around the concept of trauma' (2008: 28).

Lauren Berlant contends that

> the public rhetoric of citizen trauma has become so pervasive and competitive in the United States that it obscures basic differences among modes of identity, hierarchy and violence. Mass national pain threatens to turn into banality, a crumbling archive of dead signs and tired plots.
>
> (1997: 2)

Berlant here describes what Mark Seltzer has defined as 'the pathological public sphere', an arena that 'represents itself to itself, from the art and culture scenes to tabloid and talk TV, as a culture of suffering, states of injury, and wounded attachments' (1997: 4). Seltzer attributes the emergence of the pathological public sphere to 'the resurgence of the category of "the trauma"' (1997: 4) in the late twentieth century. He reads the revival of trauma as the defining characteristic of a 'wound culture' that exhibits 'a public fascination with torn and opened bodies and torn and opened persons, a collective gathering around shock, trauma, and the wound' (1997: 4). As Seltzer expands, this wound culture exists at the intersection of 'the vague and shifting lines between the singularity and privacy of the subject, on the one side, and collective forms of representation, exhibition, and witnessing, on the other' (1997: 4). Contemporary wound culture internalizes and institutionalizes all of the conceptual slippages that have characterized the discussion of trauma throughout this chapter: eliding bodily and psychological suffering, conflating the experiences of individuals and collectives, and collapsing the distinction between private and public spheres.

So what historical conditions would account for the emergence of a wound culture and its attendant pathologies? Kirby Farrell suggests that late-twentieth-century America was characterized by 'a post-traumatic mood' that came as 'an aftershock of the great catastrophes of midcentury' (1998: 2). As the traumas of the Great Depression and the Second World War were compounded by 'the Cold War, the Korean War, McCarthyism, threats of nuclear annihilation, and new racial and socioeconomic tensions', Farrell argues, Americans felt 'a disturbance in the ground of collective experience' (1998: 2–3). New anxieties about 'loss of control and decline or degeneration' (1998: 3) were heightened by social and environmental crises from the AIDS epidemic to climate change. Cumulatively, these events were registered as 'a shock to people's values, trust and sense of purpose; an obsessive awareness that nations, leaders, even we ourselves can die' (1998: 3).

Farrell thus contends that 'trauma is … psychocultural' (1998: 7): it is socially defined, mediated, and constructed, and its parameters are continually mutating. As its *Oxford English Dictionary* (2000) entry makes clear, the popular understanding of trauma has moved from physical injury (in the eighteenth and nineteenth centuries), to psychical injury (in the late nineteenth and early twentieth centuries), to a description of general experiential unpleasantness (from the late twentieth century onwards). Over the course of these transitions, the definition of trauma has paradoxically become both more and less specific. The intense scrutiny to which trauma has been subjected has allowed it to be more clearly defined in clinical terms. However, as it has gained cultural currency in vernacular parlance, the notion of trauma has been emptied of much of its meaning and indiscriminately applied to a seemingly limitless range of experiences. As Farrell notes, today

> trauma is both a clinical syndrome and a trope something like the Renaissance figure of the world as a stage: a strategic fiction that a complex, stressful society is using to account for a world that seems threateningly out of control.
>
> (1998: 2)

Through its transvaluation as political, economic, and social capital in the late twentieth century, trauma has emerged as a defining sign of contemporary subjectivity and solidified into a cultural master narrative. As this chapter has aimed to demonstrate, the emergence of trauma as a cornerstone of today's society should not merely be regarded as the inevitable consequence of the new pathologies produced by modernity, but as a direct result of the ideological and epistemological frameworks that have guided the scientific, political, economic, and cultural institutions that have sought to manage and mitigate these developments. Moving away from the field of clinical inquiry, the following chapters will chart the ways in which trauma has entered other areas of academic interest, focusing particularly on the evolution of cultural trauma studies from the 1990s to the present.

2

WORDS FOR WOUNDS

In the course of the 1990s, trauma moved from being an object of clinical inquiry to a preoccupation among literary and cultural scholars. This chapter aims to account for the emergence of trauma theory as a humanistic field of inquiry by tracing its roots to long-standing debates about the ethics and aesthetics of representing the Holocaust and a more recent paradigm shift in literary studies that created favourable conditions for an interest in trauma to blossom. After discussing these intellectual and institutional factors, we will sketch the contours of literary trauma theory by introducing the work of some of its founding figures.

POETRY AFTER AUSCHWITZ

To suggest that trauma and literature, or art more generally, are intimately intertwined and even inextricably bound up with one another, as literary trauma theory does, is to make a provocative and controversial claim. After all, it has long been the established view that literature and (especially historical) trauma do not have anything to do with one another; or, at least, that they *should* not have anything to do with one another. People who take the view that it is inappropriate for literature to engage with major historical traumas, such as the Holocaust, often invoke the support of the German Jewish Marxist philosopher and critical theorist Theodor Adorno, who, in 'Cultural Criticism and Society', an essay written in 1949 and published in 1951, famously declared that '[t]o write poetry after Auschwitz is barbaric' (1981: 34). This statement has been instrumental in creating a climate of suspicion around literary and artistic representations of the Holocaust—for which 'Auschwitz', the most notorious of all the Nazi camps, is a synecdoche—in particular and painful histories in general. As Ernst van Alphen points out, '[w]hereas up to World War II the creation of art and literature possessed a serious, almost religious aura, after Auschwitz it suddenly seemed a shockingly frivolous occupation' (1997: 17–18).

Over the years Adorno's proposition—which in the original German is not even a full sentence ('nach Auschwitz ein Gedicht zu schreiben, ist barbarisch')—has been much quoted and misquoted, appropriated and misappropriated, de- and re-contextualized by scholars working in many different contexts and disciplines. A common misreading turns it into a statement about the impossibility, rather than barbarism, of post-Holocaust poetry. Adorno is said to claim that poetry is impossible after Auschwitz, even though the complex passage in which he allegedly makes this argument actually 'predicates its existence' (Rowland 1997: 57). The view imputed to him is that silence is the only suitable response to the Holocaust. Setting the tone for many subsequent accounts, George Steiner, the French-born American literary critic who first brought Adorno's ideas about Auschwitz to an English-speaking audience, misquotes him as requesting that there be '[n]o poetry after Auschwitz' (1967: 53). Steiner wonders whether 'our civilization, by virtue of the inhumanity it has carried out and condoned', has 'forfeited its claims to that indispensable luxury which we call literature' (1967: 53) and suggests that, in the face of the Holocaust, the best thing to do is to be silent: 'Silence *is* an alternative. When the words in the city are full of savagery and lies, nothing speaks louder than an unwritten poem' (1967: 54). Invoking Adorno, he effectively calls for a ban on the writing of poetry in the post-Holocaust era, a stance that he recanted in his later work.

In the two decades following the publication of 'Cultural Criticism and Society', Adorno himself also repeatedly readdressed his oft-cited statement about poetry and Auschwitz, reiterating and revising his original formulation, and making it clear that silence is in fact not the best response in his view. In a well-known 1962 essay entitled 'Commitment', he specifies what it is about literature and art that has become inappropriate after Auschwitz. '[B]y turning suffering into images', Adorno writes, art makes us feel embarrassed in front of the victims:

> it wounds the shame we feel in the presence of the victims. For these victims are used to create something, works of art, that are thrown to the consumption of a world which destroyed them. The so-called artistic representation of the sheer physical pain of people beaten to the ground by rifle-butts contains, however remotely, the power to elicit enjoyment out of it. ... The aesthetic principle of stylization ... make[s] an unthinkable fate appear to have had some meaning; it is transfigured, something of its horror removed.
>
> (1980: 189)

He does not object, then, to literary or artistic representation as such but to transfiguration and stylization. Atrocities such as the Holocaust must not be given meaning and transformed into images and artworks from which aesthetic pleasure can be derived, as this would 'do[] an injustice to the victims' (1980: 189).

Nevertheless, Adorno contends in the same essay that literature and art are utterly indispensable. Paradoxically enough, it is only literary and artistic works that can henceforth live up to the task of doing justice to the victims by remaining true to their suffering. Adorno repeats his earlier claim about poetry after Auschwitz, which has been the subject of much intervening debate, but goes on to complicate it:

> I have no wish to soften the saying that to write lyric poetry after Auschwitz is barbaric ... But [Hans Magnus] Enzensberger's retort also remains true, that literature must resist this verdict ... [I]t is now virtually in art alone that suffering can still find its own voice, consolation, without immediately being betrayed by it.
>
> (1980: 188)

When Adorno writes that practically the only way in which we can give a voice to the pain of the victims is through art, he recognizes that '[a]esthetic experience cannot be reduced to "pleasure" in the sense of (distracting) amusement' (van Alphen 1997: 19). Objections to literary or artistic representations of major historical traumas based on Adorno's earlier statement in fact rely on 'a rather limited conception of literature and art, one restricted to sheer aesthetics in the sense of enjoyment or distraction' (1997: 19). As Adorno's later comments make clear, writing poetry after Auschwitz is not necessarily barbaric: it does not inevitably betray the victims; it may even be a unique way of keeping faith with them. Though literature and art can lead us away from the historical reality of the trauma, they are also media through which we can gain privileged access to it.

The barbarism of cultural production after the Holocaust, for Adorno, lies in its inability or refusal to acknowledge its inadequacy for representing atrocity. Rather than calling for silence, Adorno argues for art that bears witness to its own incapacity to represent the unrepresentable: 'autonomous' as distinct from representational art. As Michael Rothberg observes, while Adorno's initial statement 'seems deliberately antiaesthetic', his subsequent reformulations, and indeed most of his writings, 'refine the status of the aesthetic, granting authentic or autonomous art a role of absolute importance in articulating a critique of capitalist society' (2000: 57). Adorno's championing of the modernist writings of the Irish dramatist Samuel Beckett and the German Jewish poet Paul Celan, which in his view do manage to stay true to the memory of the Holocaust by refusing realist figuration, indicates that 'the near-silence and imagelessness of art after Auschwitz should not be confused with actual silence or with a ban on representation *tout court*' (2000: 46).

Following Adorno, intellectuals who have grappled at length with the simultaneous necessity and impossibility of representing the Holocaust include, in addition to Steiner, the French writer and literary theorist Maurice Blanchot and the French philosopher Jean-François Lyotard. Blanchot's most explicit meditations on the significance of the Holocaust date from the 1980s. In his essay 'After the Fact', in which he reflects on two of his early stories, Blanchot, echoing Adorno's dictum, writes that 'there can be no fiction-story about Auschwitz' (1999: 494). The impact of the Nazi genocide is so profound that 'all narration, even all poetry, has lost the foundation on which another language could be raised—through the extinction of the happiness of speaking that lurks in even the most mediocre silence' (1999: 494). As a result, Blanchot notes, with another nod to Adorno, '[n]o matter when it is written, every story from now on will be from before Auschwitz' (1999: 495). Unlike Steiner, though, Blanchot does not advocate silence in response to the representational impasse created by the Holocaust; rather, like Adorno, he favours a form of writing, which he both theorized and practised himself, that incorporates a self-reflexive awareness of the limits of representation; a 'writing of the disaster', to cite the title of one of his most relevant books (1986), that confronts the catastrophe by registering its inevitable failure to adequately capture and convey it.

Lyotard's thoughts on the Holocaust and representation also show the influence of Adorno. Lyotard, who famously defined the postmodern condition as a state of 'incredulity toward metanarratives' (1984: xxiv), views postmodernism as a response to the Holocaust (Eaglestone 2004: 2). 'Auschwitz', for Lyotard, is the paradigmatic event that destroyed the project of modernity and inaugurated the postmodern era (1993: 18). The Holocaust caused the grand narratives ('grands récits') of progress and rationality, which provided an all-encompassing framework for understanding the world, to lose their credibility and legitimacy, leaving only a plurality of local micronarratives ('petites histoires') in their place. In an oft-quoted passage from *The Differend: Phrases in Dispute* (1988), Lyotard compares the Holocaust to an earthquake that

> destroys not only lives, buildings, and objects but also the instruments used to measure earthquakes directly and indirectly. The impossibility of quantitatively measuring it does not prohibit, but rather inspires in the minds of the survivors the idea of a very great seismic force.
>
> (1988: 56)

He adds that

> the historian must break with the monopoly over history granted to the cognitive regimen of phrases, and he or she must venture forth by lending his or her ear to what is not presentable under the rules of knowledge.

> Every reality entails this exigency insofar as it entails possible unknown senses. Auschwitz is the most real of realities in this respect. Its name marks the confines wherein historical knowledge sees its competence impugned. It does not follow from that that one falls into non-sense.
>
> (1988: 57–58)

Lyotard presents Auschwitz as the exemplary *differend*, a term he coined to denote something that must be put into sentences but cannot be (1988: 13). He advocates for fidelity to the *differend* and the (im)possibility of phrasing it through attention to 'what is not presentable under the rules of knowledge', rather than through the continued privileging of conventional modes of understanding and representation that it exceeds.

As we will see, trauma theory stands in the tradition of Adorno, Steiner, Blanchot, and Lyotard in that it, too, arose out of an engagement with the ethical and aesthetic dilemmas involved in bearing witness to the Holocaust; it is similarly marked by an intense preoccupation with the demands of events and experiences that defy comprehension and narrativization, and invested in the idea that literature and art are somehow uniquely positioned to meet those contradictory demands. The field as it took shape in the early 1990s also has its roots, though, in a major paradigm shift that occurred in literary studies around that time, and which we will explore in the next section.

SHIFTING PARADIGMS

At the risk of oversimplification, the dominant paradigms in literary scholarship in the last quarter of the twentieth century were, in chronological order, textualism, historicism, and ethical criticism. The 1970s and the early 1980s were the heyday of poststructuralism and deconstruction, schools of thought that radicalized the notion originally espoused by structuralism, introduced by the Swiss linguist Ferdinand de Saussure, that language does not reflect meaning but creates it via a system of differences. Deconstruction, which became particularly influential in literary studies, is an approach to the study of texts, both literary and philosophical, that is concerned with the ways in which texts resist being reduced to a coherent and consistent meaning that is *the* meaning of the text. Its focus is on the resistant materiality of the text, which produces not *one* meaning, nor a happy plurality of multiple meanings, but a number of strictly incompatible meanings that leave the reader faced with the experience of undecidability. It is mainly associated with the work of the French philosopher Jacques Derrida and that of various literary scholars at Yale University, most prominently Paul de Man, Geoffrey Hartman, J. Hillis Miller, and Harold Bloom.

This paradigm came under attack in the course of the 1980s. Because of its preoccupation with textuality, deconstruction was accused of being indifferent and irrelevant to 'real-world' issues. Whether wilfully or not, Derrida's famous statement '*There is nothing outside of the text*' ('*il n'y a pas de hors-texte*') (1998: 158) was often misinterpreted as a blithe and irresponsible dismissal of reality, as if he were preposterously claiming that nothing exists beyond language, whereas in actual fact it means that we have no unmediated access to reality. Cathy Caruth notes the pervasiveness of these kinds of concerns in her introduction to the 1995 collection *Critical Encounters: Reference and Responsibility in Deconstructive Writing*:

> In recent years, the questions raised by poststructuralist criticism, and particularly deconstruction, concerning the establishment of reference have seemed to many readers to involve a dangerous denial of any link between texts and reality: the possibility that reference is indirect seems to mean that we have no reliable access to experience or to history and hence no basis for political action or ethical decision.
>
> (1995c: 1)

Around the mid-1980s, textualism, increasingly maligned and marginalized, was eclipsed by new historicism, cultural materialism, cultural studies, postcolonialism, feminism, gay and lesbian studies, and Marxist criticism. These approaches were often indebted to poststructuralism but claimed to be more attentive to history and politics, which the previous paradigm was criticized for ignoring or overlooking due to its allegedly excessive emphasis on language.

A major contributing factor to this paradigm shift was the so-called de Man affair, which broke out in 1987 and rocked the world of literary criticism to its core, prompting a re-evaluation of the ethics of deconstruction. The Belgian-born literary critic and theorist Paul de Man, who had died in 1983, was the most admired and influential exponent of the Yale school of deconstruction, which applied Derrida's ideas to the reading of literary texts. The affair that bears his name concerns the discovery by a Belgian PhD student, Ortwin de Graef, currently an English literature professor at the University of Leuven, of a number of articles published by the young de Man in 1941 and 1942 in the collaborationist press in Nazi-occupied Belgium. De Man's wartime journalism turned out to contain anti-Semitic passages, which not only led to accusations that he had been a Nazi sympathizer in his youth, but also retrospectively encouraged a suspicion that the mode of analysing literary texts that he had developed and championed in later life was complicit in Nazi ideology. As one later observer puts it, somewhat hyperbolically (and with a nod to Virginia Woolf): 'On or about December 1, 1987 [the day the *New York Times* broke the news on its front page], the nature of literary theory changed' (Harpham 1999: 20). The revelations about de Man's murky past gave opponents of deconstruction new ammunition with which to attempt to discredit and finish off a paradigm that was already in decline. Deconstruction was alleged to have been exposed as integrally bound to the worldview of national socialism. Instead of being merely indifferent to what goes on in the real world, it now stood accused of being actually immoral. In the aftermath of the de Man scandal, critics rushed to declare the death of deconstruction.

However, rumours of deconstruction's demise turned out to have been greatly exaggerated, as trauma theory soon appeared upon the scene, giving it a new lease of life. In the early 1990s, several literary scholars who shared a background in deconstruction and an affiliation with the Yale school—Caruth, Hartman, and Shoshana Felman—turned their attention to trauma in an effort to redeem and rehabilitate a mode of criticism that had fallen out of favour. Trauma theory as they conceived it could be usefully understood as the reinvention in an ethical guise of an embattled paradigm struggling to reclaim the dominant position it once held by insisting on its relevance to history. Caruth opens the first chapter of her seminal 1996 book *Unclaimed Experience: Trauma, Narrative, and History*, one of the founding texts of the field, by pitting 'the peculiar and paradoxical experience of trauma' against the argument that post-structuralist criticism denies us access to history and thereby deprives us of any basis for ethical or political judgement (1996: 11).

Indeed, the central claim of Caruth's brand of trauma theory is that aligning a psychoanalytic view of trauma with a deconstructive vigilance regarding the indeterminacies of representation in the analysis of texts that bear witness to trauma can grant us a paradoxical mode of access to extreme events and experiences that defy understanding and representation. Trauma theory thus effectively sought to reconcile the textualist and historicist approaches to the study of literary texts, showing that the perceived gap between them was not unbridgeable after all. If poststructuralism had ostensibly driven the real underground, it resurfaced as the traumatic event in the 1990s. In this account, textual undecidability or unreadability came to reflect the inaccessibility of trauma. As Ana Douglass and Thomas Vogler point out,

> The traumatic event bears a striking similarity to the always absent signified or referent of the poststructuralist discourse, an object that can by definition only be constructed retroactively, never observed directly ... This combination of the simultaneous undeniable reality of the traumatic event with its unapproachability offers the possibility for a seeming reconciliation between the undecidable text and the ontological status of the traumatic event as an absolute signified.
>
> (2003: 5)

A reading practice that attends to the breakdown of meaning thus becomes charged with ethical significance as a privileged form of witnessing.

Trauma theory can be contextualized as one manifestation of a larger 'ethical turn' that swept through literary studies, and the humanities more generally, in the 1990s, partly but not exclusively in response to the de Man affair. It was around this time also that Anglo-American moral philosophers such as Martha Nussbaum, Richard Rorty, and Charles Taylor began to show a conspicuous interest in literature. According to David Parker, the turn towards the ethical within literary studies was 'closely connected to', and even 'fuelled primarily by', this 'turn to the literary within ethics'

(1998: 14). The central figure here was Nussbaum, who made an influential case for the importance of the literary imagination in moral philosophy and public life in her books *Love's Knowledge* (1990) and *Poetic Justice* (1995). Literature exerts a beneficial moral influence on the reader, according to Nussbaum, by exercising his or her imagination and bringing him or her into close contact with the complexity of the lives of others.

The neo-humanist variety of literary-ethical inquiry practised by Nussbaum and her followers concentrated on the growth of the self as a moral being. However, the ethical paradigm that came to the fore in the 1990s also included a deconstructive variant, of which trauma theory is a sub-strand, that emphasized the need to respect otherness and resist its reduction to sameness. Taking their cue from the work of the French philosopher Emmanuel Levinas and the revisions of his thought proposed by Derrida, literary scholars such as Geoffrey Harpham, Derek Attridge, J. Hillis Miller, and Robert Eaglestone focused on how to avoid the closure of meaning and preserve a space for a non-appropriative textual encounter with otherness.

Some have discerned an ethical turn in Derrida's own later writings, including *Specters of Marx* (1994), *The Gift of Death* (1995), and *The Politics of Friendship* (1997), which directly address major moral, social, and political issues such as law and justice, democracy, hospitality, friendship, forgiveness, the death penalty, and terrorism. Others, though, including Derrida himself, disagree with the marking of any particular moment in which his thought suddenly became interested in questions of ethical and political responsibility. Stressing continuity rather than discontinuity, they contend that, despite frequent accusations of frivolity, relativism, and irresponsibility or worse, deconstruction has always been engaged with the world and impelled by an ethical imperative. A concern with ethics and politics is said to have been embedded deep within the project of deconstruction since Derrida's early work, which, like the work of the theorists discussed in the previous section, responded to the shattering experience of the Holocaust. In fact, Derrida states in an interview that '[t]he thought of the incineration (*brûle-tout*) of the holocaust, of cinders, runs through all my texts' (1992: 211), and that '"Auschwitz" has obsessed everything that I have ever been able to think' (1992: 212). Eaglestone concurs that 'the Holocaust is *all-*

pervasive in Derrida's work' and argues that deconstruction 'stems from' the Holocaust (2004: 280). Far from constituting a radically new departure, then, the overt preoccupation with bearing witness to the Nazi genocide and other atrocities displayed by trauma theory would only make explicit concerns that had been at least implicit in, and very much at the heart of, deconstruction all along.

CARUTH'S UNCLAIMED EXPERIENCE

The founding work on trauma that emerged from Yale University in the early 1990s, which largely shaped the contours of the humanistic study of trauma for the next two decades and beyond, deserves closer scrutiny. The central figures here are Caruth, Felman, and Hartman, as well as the psychiatrist and psychoanalyst Dori Laub. Felman was a professor of French and comparative literature at Yale until she moved to Emory University in 2004. Hartman was a close colleague of de Man's in the Yale English Department, and he co-founded what is now the Fortunoff Video Archive for Holocaust Testimonies at Yale with Laub in the early 1980s. Caruth studied with de Man and Hartman, completing her PhD under the latter's supervision in 1988. In the preface to the monograph that resulted from it three years later, *Empirical Truths and Critical Fictions: Locke, Wordsworth, Kant, Freud*, she acknowledges her indebtedness to these two tutelary presences (1991: ix). Caruth taught at Yale until, like Felman, she took up a position at Emory, in 1994.

Caruth's extremely influential contribution to the formation of trauma studies in the 1990s comes in the shape of the introductions she wrote for two guest-edited special issues of the journal *American Imago* on 'Psychoanalysis, Culture and Trauma', published in 1991 and republished as an essay collection under the title *Trauma: Explorations in Memory* in 1995, and the short monograph *Unclaimed Experience: Trauma, Narrative, and History*, which appeared in 1996. In *Trauma: Explorations in Memory*, Caruth, drawing on the DSM definition, describes trauma as follows:

> While the precise definition of post-traumatic stress disorder is contested, most descriptions generally agree that there is a response, sometimes delayed, to an overwhelming event or events, which takes

> the form of repeated, intrusive hallucinations, dreams, thoughts or behaviors stemming from the event, along with numbing that may have begun during or after the experience, and possibly also increased arousal to (and avoidance of) stimuli recalling the event.
>
> (1995a: 4)

She goes on to draw attention to the 'very peculiar fact', implicit in this definition, that the pathology in question cannot be defined by 'the event itself' nor in terms of 'a *distortion* of the event'; it consists, rather, solely in 'the *structure of its experience* or reception: the event is not assimilated or experienced fully at the time, but only belatedly, in its repeated *possession* of the one who experiences it' (1995a: 4). It is the very unassimilated nature of trauma, the way it was not known in the first instance, that returns to haunt the survivor later on. The truth of traumatic experience, which forms the centre of its pathology, is 'a gap that carries the force of the event and does so precisely at the expense of simple knowledge and memory' (1995a: 7). In other words, the force of the experience is registered in 'the collapse of its understanding' (1995a: 7).

There is no special kind of event, then, that provokes a traumatized reaction: it is not the event itself, but rather the mental experiencing of it, that constitutes the psychological trauma. The traumatic experience of one person may not be shared by another, even in identical situations. Where many people experience the same event, only some may develop a trauma connected to it. Indeed, survivors of even the most potentially traumatizing experiences, such as imprisonment in concentration camps or genocide, do not in each and every case develop PTSD. Furthermore, it is possible for individuals to undergo a form of traumatization—through the manifestation of symptomatic effects such as extreme anxiety, panic attacks, or recurrent nightmares—even though they have not actually experienced the traumatizing event with which these effects are associated. As the following chapter illustrates, secondary or vicarious trauma has been diagnosed in the therapists and family members of PTSD sufferers, who come into contact with trauma victims over a prolonged period. Literary examples of this phenomenon can be found in such well-known texts as Art Spiegelman's comic book *Maus* (1986; 1991) and Toni Morrison's novel *Beloved* (1987), which show

how the effects of the trauma suffered by survivors of the Holocaust and slavery, respectively, are passed down to members of the next generation who did not experience the traumatizing events themselves. Secondary traumatization may even occur, though, in those reacting only to representations of trauma, such as the spectacular footage of the 9/11 attacks shown on TV or many trauma novels and films, which, as we will see, not only depict traumatizing events but can also embody and reproduce the trauma for the reader or viewer through their form of narration. The key issue to be borne in mind here is that there is no indissoluble link between trauma and event: one can live through what is held to be a traumatizing event without being traumatized, and one can be traumatized (manifest post-traumatic symptoms) without living through such an event.

The specificity of trauma resides, rather, in the fact that it is not assimilated by consciousness, not fully experienced as it occurs, which is why it returns to haunt the survivor later on, possessing them instead of being possessed by them as an 'ordinary' memory. In Caruth's model of trauma, the immediacy of the experience precludes its registration, so that it exceeds the individual's capacity for understanding. The fundamental paradox of trauma, according to Caruth, is that 'the greatest confrontation with reality may also occur as an absolute numbing to it'; that 'immediacy ... may take the form of belatedness' (1995a: 6). Registration is only possible belatedly, which means that it involves latency, a temporal delay, as postulated by Sigmund Freud. Drawing on his work, Caruth highlights the unique temporality of trauma, which had preoccupied Freud throughout his career. Caruth focuses on his later writings, particularly *Beyond the Pleasure Principle* (1920; see Freud 2010a) and *Moses and Monotheism* (1939; see Freud 2010b), which represent a break with his earlier work on the role of fantasy, dreams, and wish-fulfilment in the etiology of trauma. As we saw in the previous chapter, following the First World War and the epidemic of 'war neuroses' stemming from it, Freud found himself forced to revise these earlier theories and reconsider the significance of external events to the question of trauma. He observed that the returning soldiers suffered from nightmares that literally repeated the horrors of the war, making them relive their combat experiences against their will. Finding it impossible to understand these dreams in terms of wish-fulfilment or unconscious meaning, Freud recognized a repetition compulsion, a compulsion to return to the scene of violence and experience the horror as if for the first time. He also diagnosed this condition in victims of train accidents, who would walk away as if unharmed, only to develop a traumatic neurosis belatedly. It is not a case, according to Caruth, of repression, of an experience being registered, forgotten, and then returning; rather, there is 'an inherent latency within the experience itself' (1995a: 8). Caruth's key innovation is to bring out and emphasize this structural latency of trauma, which she infers from Freud's work.

The paradox entailed by traumatic experience as outlined by Caruth, that 'the most direct seeing of a violent event may occur as an absolute inability to know it' (1996: 91–92), poses a challenge: though the phenomenon of trauma 'urgently demands historical awareness', it 'denies our usual modes of access to it' (1995b: 151). The split within the immediate experience of trauma—its lack of integration into consciousness—means that it cannot be represented and communicated in any straightforward manner. Caruth finds support for her claim that trauma is not fully experienced as it occurs and therefore insistently returns in its exactness or literality at a later time in the neurobiological research of Bessel van der Kolk and Onno van der Hart, which itself harks back to the writing of Pierre Janet. Van der Kolk and van der Hart argue that a traumatic event elides its normal encoding in memory; it is stored differently and hence cannot become what Janet terms a 'narrative memory' that is integrated into the individual's life-story. For Janet, the goal of therapy is to convert 'traumatic memory', which merely repeats the past and is removed from conscious awareness and voluntary control, into 'narrative memory', which narrates the past as past. However, Caruth warns that the transformation of the trauma into a narrative memory 'may lose both the precision and the force that characterizes traumatic recall' (1995b: 153). Integrating the trauma into a story that can be readily understood is to deny 'the event's essential incomprehensibility, the force of its *affront to understanding*' (1995b: 154). Harmonizing narratives, stories that literally make sense of trauma, are inadequate because they fail to capture the unique specificity of a traumatic historical reality.

According to Caruth, however, '[t]he impossibility of a comprehensible story … does not necessarily mean the denial of a transmissible truth' (1995b: 154). It is not because trauma cannot be narrativized in any simple manner that its specific truth cannot be conveyed. Caruth suggests that this truth may be transmitted 'through the refusal of a certain framework of understanding, a refusal that is also a creative act of listening' (1995b: 154). Instead of a denial of knowledge of the past, the act of refusal may be a way of gaining access to knowledge that has not yet attained the form of a narrative memory. She argues that, '[i]n its active resistance to the platitudes of knowledge, this refusal opens up the space for a testimony that can speak beyond what is already understood' (1995b: 155). What we need, according to Caruth, is a kind of speech that does not simply communicate that which is understandable but also that which cannot be understood; a kind of speech that, insofar as it 'exceeds simple understanding', creates the possibility of 'a truly historical transmission' (1995b: 156).

This is where literature can be of service. For Caruth, as for Felman and Hartman, as we will see below, literature might just be that kind of speech. Caruth argues that literary language stands out in its capacity to transmit that which resists ordinary memory and understanding, and which therefore cannot be communicated in more straightforward ways. Trauma defies representation; it calls into question simple models of referentiality that hold that the signifier is a transparent vehicle for the signified. The same is true of literature as conceived by deconstructionists: unlike other forms of language, literary language is free of the fallacy of unmediated expression. It acknowledges and exploits the divergence between signifier and signified by flaunting its rhetoricity, its use of figurative language, its linguistic particularities. It is this feature, according to Caruth and like-minded critics, that makes literature eminently suited to the task of bearing witness to trauma. An event that defies all representation will best be represented by a failure of representation. What is called for, then, is the disruption of conventional modes of representation—which can be found in literature. Caruth's reflections on the inscription of trauma in language reveal the shaping influence of de Man on her thinking, which is arguably as profound as Freud's; indeed, Caruthian trauma theory basically articulates Freudian psychoanalysis with de Manian deconstruction. *Unclaimed Experience* includes a chapter theorizing trauma in terms of de Man's deconstructive critique of referentiality and suggests that 'the figure of falling' central to his late work may be 'de Man's own translation of the concept … of trauma' (1996: 7).

Caruth insists on the ethical value of bearing witness to trauma. She argues that trauma can create the grounds for new forms of community by building a bridge between disparate historical experiences. She puts forward the 'new kind of listening' to which trauma challenges us as the key to 'passing out' of the 'isolation' imposed by the traumatic event:

> This speaking and this listening—a speaking and a listening *from the site of trauma*—does not rely, I would suggest, on what we simply know of each other, but on what we don't yet know of our own traumatic pasts. In a catastrophic age, that is, trauma itself may provide the very link between cultures: not as a simple understanding of the pasts of others but rather, within the traumas of contemporary history, as our ability to listen through the departures we have all taken from ourselves.
>
> (1995a: 11)

The appeal to a 'we' that needs to open up and resituate its understanding makes it clear that trauma urges us to change not just our notion of history but also our involvement in each other's histories. Caruth further elaborates on the ethical function of bearing witness to trauma in *Unclaimed Experience*, when she argues that it is the

> plea by an other who is asking to be seen and heard … that … constitutes the new mode of reading and listening that both the language of trauma, and the silence of its mute repetition of suffering, profoundly and imperatively demand.
>
> (1996: 9–10)

With its principled refusal to appropriate or impose closure on that which is addressed to our understanding but can never be reduced to it, trauma theory issues a call for us to rethink our engagement with otherness and to develop new and more just ways of being with others.

Caruth followed up *Unclaimed Experience* with another slender monograph on trauma and literature, *Literature in the Ashes of History,* in 2013, and a collection of interviews, *Listening to Trauma: Conversations with Leaders in the Theory and Treatment of Catastrophic Experience,* one year later. In *Literature in the Ashes of History,* she returns to the relation between trauma and history, casting the latter in terms of disappearance: as the back cover blurb puts it, the book investigates 'the enigma of a history that, in its very unfolding, seems to be slipping away before our grasp'. This formulation is consonant with her focus on what she called 'unclaimed experience' in the previous book. Remarkably, Caruth's recent work barely strays from the theoretical foundations laid in her seminal earlier writings on trauma. In fact, with the notable exception of an afterword to the twentieth-anniversary edition of *Unclaimed Experience* that came out in 2016, it hardly engages with the major debates and critiques that her claims have provoked since the early 1990s. We will go into these in the next two chapters.

HARTMAN'S TRAUMATIC KNOWLEDGE

The translation of deconstruction into trauma theory that characterizes Caruth's work from the 1990s can also be traced across the scholarship of her mentor, Hartman, which underwent a similar reorientation at around the same time. While Hartman is unquestionably a founding figure of trauma theory, his work is less frequently cited and invoked than that of Caruth or Felman and Laub, in part, no doubt, because of its reticent, circumspect, or undemonstrative quality. Hartman's tendency to avoid making definite assertions and firm statements has resulted in homage and indifference becoming the predominant modes of critical (dis)engagement with his oeuvre (Vermeulen 2010: 5), with Pieter Vermeulen's sustained and systematic exegesis of it being a rare and welcome exception.

Since the beginning of his career in the 1950s, Hartman's focus had been on European Romanticism, and particularly the poetry of William Wordsworth, with which he continued to engage until his death in 2016. A key early publication is the monograph *Wordsworth's Poetry, 1787–1814,* from 1964. Trained in New Criticism, the formalist movement that dominated American literary studies in the mid-twentieth century, Hartman became one of the pivotal figures of American deconstruction in the 1970s, introducing and explicating Derrida's work, adapting it for use as literary theory, and reinterpreting English Romantic poetry through this lens. However, like Bloom, Hartman was less of a card-carrying member of the Yale school of deconstruction than de Man or Miller. His scholarship from this period is best exemplified by the volumes *Criticism in the Wilderness: The Study of Literature Today* (1980) and *Saving the Text: Literature/Derrida/Philosophy* (1981). From the 1980s onwards, starting with his involvement with the video archive for Holocaust survivor testimonies at Yale, Hartman played a central role in the fields of trauma theory and Holocaust studies. There is an autobiographical dimension to the latter interest, as the young Hartman had escaped the Nazi genocide by being evacuated from Germany, the country of his birth, on a *Kindertransport* to England, an experience he recounts in his memoir *A Scholar's Tale: Intellectual Journey of a Displaced Child of Europe* (2007), which also describes his friendship with de Man and others. Much of Hartman's work in this area—contained in books such as *The Longest Shadow: In the Aftermath of the Holocaust* (1996)—deals with Holocaust video testimony, which he conceived as an update of Wordsworth's poetical practice for a visual age.

Vermeulen, who maps Hartman's reorientations and reinventions of his project across his work in his book *Geoffrey Hartman: Romanticism after the Holocaust* (2010), detects a great deal of common ground between Hartman's scholarship on Wordsworth from the late 1970s onwards and his work on trauma and the memory of the Holocaust, on which Hartman embarked in the 1980s. Vermeulen regards the latter as 'perfectly continuous with Hartman's "mature" interpretations of Wordsworth' (2010: 4). Indeed, he sees a 'persistent commitment to a Wordsworthian ethic and aesthetic' (2010: 5) as characteristic of Hartman's project. What allowed Hartman 'to carry over his concern with English Romantic poetry into his engagement with the memory of disaster', according to Vermeulen, is his 'reliance on a rhetoric of trauma and loss' throughout his work (2010: 5).

Hartman himself reflects on this thread running through his career in two publications from the mid-1990s in which he situates his work in relation to the then-fledgling field of trauma studies. In his essay 'On Traumatic Knowledge and Literary Studies', he associates trauma, which marks 'the disjunction between experiencing … and understanding', with figurative language (1995: 540). He posits the existence of a traumatic kind of knowledge, 'one that cannot be made entirely conscious, in the sense of being fully retrieved or communicated without distortion' (1995: 537). He sees traumatic knowledge, which is 'as close to nescience as to knowledge', as consisting of 'two contradictory elements':

> One is the traumatic event, registered rather than experienced. It seems to have bypassed perception and consciousness, and falls directly into the psyche. The other is a kind of memory of the event, in the form of a perpetual troping of it by the bypassed or severely split (dissociated) psyche. On the level of poetics, literal and figurative may correspond to these two types of cognition.
>
> (1995: 537)

Hartman cites several examples of figurations of trauma that he finds in the poetry of William Blake, Samuel Taylor Coleridge, John Keats, and, in particular, Wordsworth. Their work is punctuated by moments of rupture and negativity (such as the 'mute, insensate things' in Wordsworth's Lucy poems) but, he argues, holds out the possibility of recovery and transmission: 'everything works against trauma in Wordsworth, yet the basis of trauma is there' (Caruth and Hartman 1996: 638). Hartman relates trauma studies to what he sees as a wider drive within the profession of literary criticism 'to make the literary object of study more transitive, more connected with what goes on in a blatantly political world' (1995: 543). Through its focus on disclosing 'an unconscious or not-knowing knowledge', which he labels 'a potentially literary way of knowing', trauma studies provides such a transition to a real world that cannot be known 'as such' due to its traumatic nature (1995: 544). In an interview conducted by Caruth in 1996, whose point of departure is her observation of 'a possible continuity' in his career centring on 'the intricate relation between what he calls "literary knowledge" and the various forms of traumatic loss', Hartman elaborates on these claims (Caruth and Hartman 1996: 631). He acknowledges his abiding interest in defining 'a specifically literary knowledge, which can reveal without full consciousness, or systematic analysis' (1996: 632), and explicitly links this with trauma as theorized by Caruth: 'the "unclaimed experience", as you call it, can only be reclaimed by literary knowledge' (1996: 641).

While already touched upon in the aforementioned essay, the ethical import of the kind of work that literature does as a privileged medium for bearing witness to trauma is fully spelled out in Hartman's book *The Fateful Question of Culture* from 1997. There he makes the uncharacteristically strong and startling claim that Wordsworth's poetic intervention in the transition from a traditional, rural society to a modern, industrialized one can be credited with guarding England from national socialism and thus preventing an English Holocaust. Hartman speculates that, by managing this transition in such a way as to prevent traumatization, Wordsworth's mediation 'saved English politics from the virulence of a nostalgic political ideal centering on rural virtue, which led to serious ravages on the continent' (1997: 7). While Hartman claims 'no more than heuristic value' for his rather breathtaking thesis, in the next sentence he turns it into an article of faith:

> But were my conjectures to be disproved or shown incapable of being proved, I would continue to feel as Mrs. Henshaw does, in Willa Cather's *My Mortal Enemy*: 'How the great poets shine on ... ! Into all the dark corners of the world. They have no night'.
>
> (1997: 7)

What sustains Hartman's assertion that Wordsworth's poetry helped England resist the temptations that resulted in genocidal outcomes in mainland Europe are particular features of Wordsworth's mode of literary representation. As Vermeulen points out, Hartman's interpretations of Wordsworth from the late 1970s on emphasize that the poet accomplishes two things at the same time: 'first, his poetry instigates a deepened awareness of loss, of the fact that things can disappear ... ; second, Wordsworth's poetry simultaneously affirms the reality of something that remains untouched by loss' (2010: 89–90). As conceived by Hartman, Wordsworth's aesthetic operation 'makes possible an experience of non-experience' by giving a reality that we cannot confront directly a form that we can experience and remember (2010: 102). It thus allows for a distinct kind of mourning that 'loosens our melancholic attachment to loss' while 'counteract[ing] mourning's tendency to abstract from the particularity of loss' (2010: 101).

The momentous cultural impact Hartman ascribes to Wordsworth—warding off genocidal violence—has a contemporary equivalent, or so Hartman hopes, in the beneficial effect allegedly produced by Holocaust video testimonies, with which he became preoccupied in the 1980s as a co-founder of Yale's Fortunoff Video Archive, and on which he published extensively (besides *The Longest Shadow*, see, for example, his essays 'The Humanities of Testimony', 'Memory.com', and 'Shoah and Intellectual Witness'). Indeed, Hartman tends to theorize that genre as 'a contemporary instantiation of Wordsworth's saving mediation' (Vermeulen 2011: 552–53). As Vermeulen explains,

> For Hartman, the domination of the visual media endangers access to history and to whatever resists full visualization, and it also contributes to the erosion of experience ... Hartman proposes the genre of video testimony as a cultural force that can counter such neutralization and that can restore the possibility of a genuine experience of non-presence.
> (2010: 116)

By adopting a 'counter-cinematic' representational mode—'us[ing] television to cure television, to turn the medium against itself, limiting while exploiting its visualizing power'—video testimony respects the reality of what resists visualization and provides an occasion for the experience of non-experience (Hartman 2000: 9). In a media-saturated world, video testimony safeguards the possibility of genuine experience. Hence the parallel between Wordsworth's past achievement and the promise of video testimony today.

FELMAN AND LAUB'S CRISES OF WITNESSING

Video testimony also plays a prominent role in Felman and Laub's *Testimony: Crises of Witnessing in Literature, Psychoanalysis, and*

History, whose publication in 1992 was a landmark moment in the establishment of trauma studies as a field. The book's impact rivals that of Caruth's publications from the same period in terms of setting the agenda for humanistic trauma scholarship for decades to come. In fact, it does not make much sense to see these scholars' respective contributions as neatly separated from each other. Two chapters from *Testimony*, one by Felman and one by Laub, had been included in a special issue of *American Imago* guest-edited by Caruth in the previous year and republished in *Trauma: Explorations in Memory* in 1995. Moreover, Caruth's thinking bears clear traces of Felman and Laub's (as well as Hartman's) influence, and Felman and Laub in turn thank Caruth for her input in the acknowledgements section of their book. While they each have their own unique perspective, these scholars openly recognize that they have learnt from each other. Trauma studies as it emerged in the early 1990s is very much a collective endeavour, the product of a vibrant intellectual environment conducive to the cross-fertilization of ideas rather than the creation of single minds working in splendid isolation.

Testimony marks the transformation of deconstruction into trauma theory in the work of Felman, another Yale critic, who until then was most famous for her ingenious 1977 essay on Henry James's *The Turn of the Screw* (1898). In a tour-de-force analysis, Felman, taking her cue from Derridean deconstruction as well as from Lacanian psychoanalysis, argues that readers of James's novella—about a governess who, caring for two children at a remote country home, becomes convinced that the estate is haunted—are frustrated in their attempts to understand the governess or her story. Felman explores how *The Turn of the Screw* generates ambiguity, emphasizing not 'the text's meaning' but rather 'that through which meaning in the text *does not come off*, that which in the text, and through which the text, *fails to mean*, that which can engender but *a conflict of interpretations*' (1977: 112). By the early 1990s, Felman was still concerned to expose the instability of meaning, but her focus shifted from literary and philosophical texts to Holocaust testimony—a research object of great interest also to Laub, her co-author, a Holocaust survivor himself and a co-founder of Yale's Fortunoff Video Archive for Holocaust Testimonies. Moreover, as we saw with Caruth and Hartman, Felman's analytical practice assumed a new sense of urgency and gravity, as studying testimony became tantamount to doing justice to history and honouring the memory of its victims. Containing chapters—signed by either Felman or Laub—on a variety of different literary, visual, artistic, and autobiographical testimonial texts, *Testimony* interprets the Holocaust as 'a radical historical *crisis of witnessing*, and as the unprecedented, inconceivable, historical occurrence of "an event without a witness"—an event eliminating its own witness' (Felman and Laub 1992: xvii).

This being the case, it falls to literature and art, once again, to give us access to this traumatic reality, which cannot otherwise be witnessed. Felman and Laub introduce their study as 'a book about how art inscribes (artistically bears witness to) *what we do not yet know of our lived historical relation to events of our times*' (1992: xx). Indeed, they regard literature and art as 'a precocious mode of witnessing—of accessing reality—when all other modes of knowledge are precluded' (1992: xx). Citing the Holocaust survivor and novelist Elie Wiesel's statement that, '[i]f the Greeks invented tragedy, the Romans the epistle and the Renaissance the sonnet, … our generation invented a new literature, that of testimony' (1992: 5–6), Felman suggests that 'testimony is the literary—or discursive—mode par excellence of our times' and that 'our era can precisely be defined as the age of testimony' (1992: 5). The writers and artists whose work she discusses in *Testimony* include the French novelist and philosopher Albert Camus, the German Jewish poet Paul Celan, and Claude Lanzmann, the French director of the monumental Holocaust documentary *Shoah* (1985). Hailed as 'the work of art of our times' (1992: xix) by Felman and Laub, *Shoah* is a nine-hour film made exclusively of testimonies of survivors, perpetrators, and other witnesses of the Holocaust, interviewed and filmed by Lanzmann over an eleven-year period. Like Caruth in *Unclaimed Experience*, Felman also devotes a chapter to de Man, in which she takes up her disgraced late colleague's defence, controversially interpreting his lifelong silence about his collaborationist past as testifying to 'the impossible confession of the Holocaust' (1992: xix). Throughout the book, she resorts to by now familiar paradoxical formulations to describe the double bind between the simultaneous necessity and impossibility of bearing witness to trauma.

Among the best-known sections of *Testimony* are the opening chapters. In 'Education and Crisis, or the Vicissitudes of Teaching', Felman develops a pedagogy of witness based on her experience of teaching a course on 'Literature and Testimony' at Yale that inadvertently caused her students to undergo a form of secondary traumatization. The chapter describes the students' emotional responses to the Holocaust and other testimonial texts with which Felman confronted them: writings by Camus, Celan, Freud, the Russian novelist Fyodor Dostoevsky, and the French poet Stéphane Mallarmé, as well as video testimonies borrowed from the Fortunoff Video Archive, which elicited a particularly strong reaction. Finding that the class profoundly affected her students in ways that she had not expected, Felman reflects on the apparent crisis in the classroom instigated by the assigned readings and viewings, which 'broke the framework of the course' (Felman and Laub 1992: 55). As a result of this experience, she came to see her 'job as a teacher' as purposely seeking out this kind of disturbance, 'creating in the class the highest state of crisis that it could withstand' without, however, 'driving the students crazy' (1992: 53). She translated her classroom experience into a teaching pedagogy, issuing a call to teach through crisis. After all, without crisis, she argues, learning cannot take place:

> I would venture to propose, today, that teaching in itself, teaching as such, takes place precisely only through a crisis: if teaching does not hit upon some sort of crisis, if it does not encounter either the vulnerability or the explosiveness of a (explicit or implicit) critical and unpredictable dimension, it has perhaps *not truly taught*: it has perhaps passed on some facts, passed on some information and some documents, with which the students or the audience—the recipients—can for instance do what people during the occurrence of the Holocaust precisely did with information that kept coming forth but that no one could *recognize*, and that no one could therefore truly *learn, read* or *put to use*.
>
> (1992: 53)

In the age of testimony, teaching, for Felman, must 'make something *happen*' instead of just transmitting passive knowledge, passing on preconceived information (1992: 53). In the light of the charged debate about the need for 'trigger warnings'—messages intended to alert students that the subject matter of a class may cause them distress—that has been raging on many US campuses and elsewhere in recent years, the widespread implementation of Felman's theory of education would in all likelihood run into institutional obstacles were it to be attempted today.

The role of the audience of testimony is further explored by Laub in 'Bearing Witness or the Vicissitudes of Listening' and 'An Event without a Witness: Truth, Testimony and Survival', the two shorter chapters that immediately follow Felman's 'Education and Crisis' and the only ones in the volume authored by Laub. Representing his most notable contribution to trauma scholarship (Laub died in 2018), they focus on the role of the listener in the testimonial process. Rather than being a passive recipient, the listener, according to Laub, is 'a party to the creation of knowledge *de novo*' (1992: 57). A testimony has to be received by an empathetic listener in order for it to come into being in the first place: 'The testimony to the trauma thus includes its hearer, who is, so to speak, the blank screen on which the event comes to be inscribed for the first time' (1992: 57). The listener's empathic engagement with the witness results in vicarious traumatization: 'through his very listening, he [sic] comes to partially experience trauma in himself' (1992: 57). This, in turn, makes the listener 'a participant and a co-owner of the traumatic event' (1992: 57). Laub is quite clear, though, that the listener 'does not become the victim' by virtue of sharing his or her experience: 'he preserves his own separate place, position and perspective' (1992: 58). If Laub elevates the listener's role to that of enabler and co-creator of the testimony, he also emphasizes the survivor's inability to bear witness to his or her trauma by him- or herself, declaring that 'the trauma survivor who is bearing witness has no prior knowledge, no comprehension and no memory of what happened' (1992: 58). This view of the survivor as a helpless, inarticulate victim, crucially dependent on an empathetic listener to make sense of his or her experience, directly follows from Laub's interpretation of the Holocaust as an event without a witness. While Laub, as a psychoanalyst and an interviewer for the Fortunoff Video Archive, was primarily concerned with encounters between actual witnesses and listeners in a clinical setting or for the purpose of recording Holocaust testimonies, his insights are also relevant for students of literature as they can be applied without too much difficulty to the situation of the reader of testimonial texts. Laub's ideas can be seen to aggrandize the role of the interpreter, investing the practice of analysing testimonies with a significance far in excess of what is commonly ascribed to it, which may well account for part of their appeal to literary scholars.

Ten years after *Testimony,* Felman published another major book within the field of trauma studies. In *The Juridical Unconscious: Trials and Traumas in the Twentieth Century* (2002), she turned her attention to the close relationship between trials and traumas, which have become '*conceptually articulated*', she argued, ever since the Nuremberg trials that were convened in 1945 to prosecute the crimes of Nazi Germany 'attempted to resolve the massive trauma of the Second World War by the conceptual resources and by the practical tools of the law' (2002: 1). Previously hidden, the link between trauma and the law was brought to the fore in the twentieth century, according to Felman, as a result of three interrelated developments: the discovery of psychoanalysis and trauma, the occurrence of numerous instances of mass violence made possible by the invention of weapons of mass destruction and technologies of death, and the unprecedented use of legal instruments to cope with these events' traumatic legacies (2002: 2). *The Juridical Unconscious* revolves around an analysis of two of the most famous trials of the twentieth century, which Felman viewed as paradigmatic for thinking through the interaction between trauma and the law: the trial of the senior Nazi official Adolf Eichmann for his role in organizing the Holocaust, which took place in Jerusalem in 1961, and the trial of the former American football star O. J. Simpson for the murders of his ex-wife Nicole Brown Simpson and her friend Ron Goldman, which was held in Los Angeles in 1995. Felman contends that when the law confronts trauma, a judicial blindness ensues that inadvertently re-enacts the trauma that the trial is intended to remedy. Both the Eichmann and the Simpson trials unwittingly reproduced the structures of the trauma to which they were trying to put an end. Felman gives the example of the Holocaust survivor K-Zetnik, who suddenly fainted on the witness stand while attempting to testify at the Eichmann trial due to being re-traumatized, or so she argued, by the legal proceedings themselves. This unintentional and unknowing re-enactment of trauma perpetrated by the law in its very effort to right the wrongs of history is what Felman calls 'the juridical unconscious'.

While these reflections on trauma, law, and justice may not immediately seem to be pertinent to the study of literary and artistic works, literature does in fact figure prominently in *The Juridical Unconscious.* For example, Felman reads the Simpson trial against and through the Russian writer Leo Tolstoy's novella *The Kreutzer Sonata* (1889), which tells the story of a man who kills his wife in a jealous rage and is acquitted of the crime. She argues that 'Tolstoy precociously bears witness to the O. J. Simpson trial', just as 'Zola (and in a different way, Celan) precociously bears witness to the Eichmann trial' (2002: 9). Felman reiterates and expands on the claim she and Laub made in *Testimony* about literature providing a unique mode of access to trauma when other modes of knowledge prove ineffectual (2002: 97). In her view, the shock of the encounter with trauma gave the Eichmann and Simpson trials 'a new jurisprudential dimension' (2002: 5), as it is only in such cases that the court provides a stage for the expression of what historically has been 'expressionless', a term she borrows from the German Jewish critic and philosopher Walter Benjamin to denote 'the silence of the persecuted, the unspeakability of the trauma of oppression' (2002: 13). 'In the courtroom', Felman suggests, 'the *expressionless* turns into *storytelling*' (2002: 14). For this to happen, though, legal language has to break down and give way to literary language. While both trials under scrutiny attempted to translate trauma into legal language, it is only by exploding the legal framework and appealing to literary language that they managed to give expression to what the trial as a legal proceeding could not master. For Felman, literature can communicate the truth of trauma that eludes legal discourse, whose efforts to establish closure condemn it to repeat the trauma it tries to resolve. Literature—or the literary use of language—therefore, has a crucial role to play in the age of trials and historical traumas, as it 'do[es] justice to the trauma in a way the law does not, or cannot':

> Literature is a dimension of concrete embodiment and a language of infinitude that, in contrast to the language of the law, encapsulates not closure but precisely what in a given legal case refuses to be closed and cannot be closed. It is to this refusal of the trauma to be closed that literature does justice.
>
> (2002: 8)

The Juridical Unconscious thus affirms the strong epistemological and ethical claims for trauma literature and its study made in *Testimony*.

The work of Felman and Laub, together with that of Caruth and Hartman, laid the foundations of literary trauma theory. This chapter has contextualized their work historically by relating it to the writings of Adorno, Steiner, Blanchot, and Lyotard from the early postwar period on the ethics and aesthetics of Holocaust representation. It has also shown how trauma theory emerged more immediately in response to a paradigm shift in literary studies that saw deconstruction superseded by movements or schools allegedly more attuned to the realities of history and politics in the course of the 1980s. Decades later, the landmark publications from the early-to-mid-1990s that first put trauma theory on the map as an area of humanistic scholarship continue to exert a powerful influence on this now thriving field. However, as the following chapters will make clear, in the intervening years some of their core arguments and assumptions have been critically interrogated, and new questions and research agendas have opened up that exceed the parameters they set out.

3

TRAUMA THEORIES

Not all cultural trauma theorists unreservedly subscribe to the critical programme laid out by the field's founding figures, Cathy Caruth, Shoshana Felman, Dori Laub, and Geoffrey Hartman. The past twenty-five years have seen a series of interventions, as changing historical and intellectual circumstances have led to new perspectives on trauma. Examining the tensions that have emerged from these developments, this chapter shows the range and heterogeneity of cultural trauma theory by exploring some of the most important issues to mark the field since the late twentieth century. We begin by considering the misgivings that the historian Dominick LaCapra has expressed about what he perceives as Caruth's and Felman's excessive fixation on the symptomatic acting-out of trauma, which collapses temporal distinctions and thereby threatens to inhibit action in the present. By contrast, LaCapra stresses the need to move from acting-out (or melancholia) to working-through (or mourning), a process that restores the distinction between past, present, and future and allows for political agency. These different positions are indicative of a tension within trauma theory between those who are primarily concerned with doing justice to traumatic repetition as a sign of survival and those who seek to drive home the point that one needs to heal from trauma if one is to be able to fully re-engage with life and work towards a better tomorrow. LaCapra argues that this second possibility might be further inhibited by a tendency to conflate historical loss and structural absence. The resulting confusion can lead to both an unhealthy elevation of victimhood and the marginalization of particular traumatic events. For LaCapra, both of these scenarios enhance the potential for problematic modes of vicarious victimhood that are dependent on unreflexive processes of overidentification.

This raises the question of how we might ethically relate to the suffering of others. In recent years, the idea of secondary or vicarious witnessing has attracted much interest in cultural trauma theory as the scales over which trauma is understood to travel have been dramatically expanded by the work of Marianne Hirsch, Alison Landsberg, and E. Ann Kaplan. Claims about how trauma is transmitted between victims, between victims and therapists, between victims and family members, and between victims and the general public have proved contentious, and, as a result, transmissibility has become an important ethical concern in relation to the representation and response to trauma narratives and images. These debates have cast renewed scrutiny on the relationship between individual, collective, and cultural trauma. While trauma theorists including Sigmund Freud, Caruth, and Kai Erikson have argued that trauma affects communities in much the same way as it does individuals, others have argued that collective trauma is socially constructed. As we will see, the work of Arthur Neal, Ron Eyerman, and Jeffrey Alexander, among others, has once again highlighted the political nature of trauma and the ideological factors that shape its conceptualization.

ACTING-OUT AND WORKING-THROUGH

In the introduction to the first section of *Trauma: Explorations in Memory* (1995), Caruth explores the complex relation between crisis and survival that arises from traumatic experience. On the one hand, she notes, trauma may be construed as a sign of survival, of living on after disaster, but, on the other hand, the belated registration of the traumatizing event reveals that 'it is not only the moment of the event, but of the passing out of it that is traumatic; that *survival itself*, in other words, *can be a crisis*' (1995a: 9). Much of Caruth's career has been dedicated to exploring this crisis. As we have seen, her work examines the paradoxes of a post-traumatic voice that is 'released *through the wound*' (1996: 2):

> that addresses us in the attempt to tell us of a reality or a truth that is not otherwise available. This truth, in its delayed appearance and its belated address, cannot be linked only to what is known, but also to what remains unknown in our very actions and our language
>
> (1996: 4).

In Caruth's account, the crisis of survival is intimately bound to a second crisis, a crisis of knowledge, which compounds and entrenches the first. As 'unclaimed experience', trauma remains essentially unknowable and, by extension, irresolvable. Thus, 'the story of trauma', 'far from telling of ... the escape from a death', 'rather attests to its endless impact on a life' (1996: 7). For Caruth, trauma consists not only in having confronted death, but also in having survived it. The repetition of the traumatic experience is, then, not only an attempt to understand that one has nearly died, but also an attempt to comprehend the improbable fact of one's survival.

In their seminal book *Testimony: Crises of Witnessing in Literature, Psychoanalysis, and History* (1992), Felman and Laub appear similarly committed to a vision of trauma as an ongoing crisis of survival. They interpret the violent events of the twentieth century, and of the Second World War in particular, as 'a history which is essentially *not over*', 'but whose traumatic consequences are still actively *evolving* ... in today's political, historical, cultural and artistic scene' (Felman and Laub 1992: xiv). Felman and Laub explore a *crisis of witnessing* with two distinct manifestations: first, a *crisis of listening,* in which audiences confronted by an account of a traumatic event, whether psychiatric professionals or not, become 'uprooted and disoriented, and profoundly shaken' (1992: xvi); second, a *crisis of literature,* in which the literary text is put in the impossible situation of narrating 'a history that nonetheless remains ... at once unspeakable and inarticulable', of representing an event that 'eliminat[es] its own witness' (1992: xvii). Both of these crises perpetuate the disrupted relationship between experience and knowledge that lies at the heart of trauma, frustrating the desire for resolution at individual and collective levels.

These are highly influential ideas, which have had an enormous impact on cultural trauma studies—and, in particular, those areas of trauma theory that are most closely connected with literary studies. As we saw in Chapter 2, the complex relationship between trauma and representation has rendered the concept of trauma of particular interest to scholars of literature. However, some critics have taken issue with the notion that traumatic experience engenders an ongoing, transmissible, and potentially endless crisis of survival. Foremost among these is LaCapra, who notes that, along with Saul Friedlander, he is in the rather unusual position of being a historian working in trauma studies (2004: 106). As with Caruth, Felman, Laub, and Hartman, his initial engagement with trauma arose out of the Holocaust (1994; 1998), but he has since broadened his focus to consider the impact of trauma on narratives of history more generally (2001; 2004) and the role that violence plays in human-animal relations (2009; 2018). While LaCapra's overt interest lies in examining how trauma shapes historiography, his work widely involves the analysis of literary and cultural texts: *History and Memory after Auschwitz* (1998), for example, contains lengthy discussions of Albert Camus's novella *The Fall* (1956), Claude Lanzmann's documentary *Shoah* (1985), and Art Spiegelman's graphic novel *Maus* (1986; 1991). Indeed, LaCapra holds that, 'in trying to account for or evoke experience, history must turn to testimony, oral reports, inferences from documents such as diaries and memoirs, and a carefully framed and qualified reading of fiction and art' (2004: 132).

LaCapra is generally credited with bringing conceptual clarity to trauma theory, and his engagement with the foundational discourses discussed above seeks to do just that. The starting point of LaCapra's critique of Caruth is her alleged conflation of event and experience. As LaCapra notes, '[o]ne reason the distinction is important is that a person may take part in the event without undergoing the experience of trauma' (2004: 112–13). Conversely, as highlighted in Felman and Laub's work on witnessing, 'one may experience aspects of trauma or undergo secondary traumatization … without personally living through the traumatizing event to which such effects are ascribed' (2004: 114). In either scenario, however, '[t]he experience of trauma is … unlike the traumatizing event in that it is not punctual or datable' (2004: 118). As we have already seen, for Caruth, the compulsive repetition of traumatic experience and the indefinite reach of the post-traumatic period threaten to collapse the distinction between past, present, and future. As LaCapra notes,

> when the past is uncontrollably relived, it is as if there were no difference between it and the present. ... [O]ne experientially feels as if one were back there reliving the event, and distance between here and there, then and now collapses.
>
> (2004: 119)

LaCapra's problem with this situation is two-fold: first, that Caruth overemphasizes the degree to which the past is *literally* re-enacted in the present; second, that her model of an endlessly recurring trans-historical trauma is quasi-theological in its 'valorization … negative sacrilization or rendering sublime, of trauma' (2004: 122).

Instead of elevating trauma into something mystical, elusive, and essentially unknowable, LaCapra argues that more attention should be paid to practices that facilitate the articulation of traumatic experience and the possibility of 'allowing openings to possible futures' (2004: 118). His point of departure is similar to that of Caruth, Felman, and Laub insofar as LaCapra, too, sees in trauma a crisis of knowledge, although he approaches it somewhat differently. Instead of viewing the state of unknowing that characterizes traumatic experience as insurmountable, LaCapra allows for the possibility of overcoming or, at least, ameliorating trauma's cognitive void. He comments,

> the radically disorienting experience of trauma often involves a dissociation between cognition and affect. In brief, in traumatic experience one typically can represent numbly or with aloofness what one cannot feel, and one feels overwhelmingly what one is unable to represent.
>
> (2004: 117)

For LaCapra, the key to surviving trauma is not to surrender oneself to its endless repetitions but to find a way of reconnecting knowledge and feeling, so that the survivor can re-engage with the present and begin to look towards the future.

Drawing heavily on Freud's work on mourning and melancholia, LaCapra makes the crucial distinction between two *apparently* oppositional responses to trauma: working-through and acting-out. Freud (1917) recognizes mourning (*Trauer*) and melancholia (*Melancholie*) as mutually exclusive reactions to loss. While the mourner and the melancholic both begin with a basic denial of their loss, over time the mourner relinquishes their attachment to the lost object and is able to engage with the possibility of a future. By contrast, the melancholic maintains an ongoing, and overwhelming, attachment to the past, making it impossible for them to engage fully with the present or look to the future. LaCapra adapts Freud's model for his account of working-through and acting-out. Closely aligned to mourning, working-through involves 'the effort to articulate and rearticulate affect and representation in a manner that may never transcend, but may to some viable extent counteract … that disabling disassociation' that is caused by trauma (LaCapra 2001: 42). In other words, working-through is a process of 'gaining critical distance on [traumatic] experiences and re-contextualizing them in ways that permit a re-engagement with ongoing concerns and future possibilities' (2004: 45). By contrast, in acting-out, 'the past is performatively regenerated or relived as if it were fully present rather than represented in memory and inscription' (2014: 70). Acting-out collapses the distinction between the past and the present, and maintains 'the melancholic sentiment that, in working through the past in a manner that enables survival or reengagement in life, one is betraying those who were overwhelmed and consumed by that traumatic past' (2001: 22).

For LaCapra, working-through is one possible means of frustrating the repetition compulsion and resisting the possibility of forming a destructive attachment to the past. While he regards narrative as fundamental to the project of working-through, he cautions that 'working-through need not be understood to imply the integration or transformation of the past trauma into a seamless narrative memory or total meaning or knowledge' (2004: 121). Indeed,

> there is a sense in which, while we may work on its symptoms, trauma, once it occurs, is a cause that we cannot directly change or heal. And any notion of full redemption or salvation with respect to it … is dubious.
> (2004: 119)

While LaCapra acknowledges that trauma may never be fully resolved, he presents a challenge to Caruth's warning that

> the transformation of trauma into a narrative memory that allows the story to be verbalized and communicated, to be integrated into one's own and others' knowledge of the past, may lose both the precision and the force that characterizes traumatic recall.
>
> (1995b: 153)

LaCapra also notes that while Freud positions mourning and melancholia as oppositional processes, 'there are of course a variety of possibilities between the two … These intermediary possibilities include more or less pronounced forms of partial mourning, which is never free of the traumatic residues of the past' (1998: 196). He cautions against simply rejecting the notion of acting-out or eagerly embracing an uncritical process of working-through in a quest to live happily ever after. He notes that a limited form of acting-out 'may be intimately bound up with working through problems. But it should not be isolated, theoretically fixated on, or one-sidedly valorized as the horizon of thought or life' (1998: 185). Ultimately, then, LaCapra remains convinced that, in resisting 'the tendency to sacralize trauma or to convert it into a founding or sublime event' (2004: 123), reflexively 'working through the past is itself in good part an ethical process, and it may be most effective when it is situated in social and political contexts' (2001: 185).

HISTORICAL AND STRUCTURAL TRAUMA

As the previous quotation suggests, LaCapra's historicist training keeps him attuned to the real-world implications of cultural trauma theory. It may thus seem unsurprising that he voices a certain unease about the ahistorical implications of some of Caruth's work. LaCapra's primary complaint is that Caruth conflates discrete instances of historical loss with the foundational problem of structural absence in such a way as to universalize trauma and to frustrate any possibility of working-through. He contends that Caruth's work reveals 'the conflation of a putatively transhistorical condition of abjection with the specific problem of victimization, thereby both adding to the allure of victimhood and obscuring the status of discrete historical victims' (LaCapra 2004: 116). His concern is that this stance makes trauma seem almost desirable, allowing non-traumatized individuals to indulge in 'the confusion of imaginary or vicarious experiential identification with certain events and the belief that one actually lived through them' (2004: 118).

The origins of this conflation appear to lie in Caruth's background in deconstructive literary theory. As Lucy Bond contends, Caruth's work on trauma 'is essentially a discussion of historical experience as a form of referential collapse. The inability to "know" the traumatic event manifests itself in the failure to bear witness to it' (2015: 20). In placing trauma beyond articulation, Caruth points to a gap 'at the heart of language as the causal factor in the failure to fully articulate experience. The rending of word and world becomes the origin of a structural trauma that frustrates all attempts at historical understanding' (Bond 2015: 20). Placed outside of narrative, history itself becomes a traumatic experience and trauma 'a symptom of history' (Caruth 1995a: 5). As Caruth expands,

> For history to be a history of trauma means that it is referential precisely to the extent that it is not fully perceived as it occurs; or to put it slightly differently, that a history can be grasped only in the very inaccessibility of its occurrence.
>
> (1996: 18)

By conflating structural and historical trauma in this way, Caruth blurs the distinction between the endemic referential failure that is the focus of poststructuralist theory and the specific psychological consequences of particular historical catastrophes. This model has the effect of lending trauma a viral agency that spreads via the language community. Like Felman and Laub, Caruth argues that trauma produces a crisis of listening in which the traumatized subject struggles with the impossible task of adequately testifying to their experience before a witness who is 'devoid of potential interpretative agency and has become the mere carrier of trauma' (Crownshaw 2010: 6). In Caruth's terms,

> To listen to the crisis of a trauma ... is not only to listen for the event, but to hear in testimony the survivor's departure from it; the challenge of the therapeutic listener, in other words, is *how to listen to departure*.
>
> (Caruth 1995a: 10)

As the subject 'departs' from their trauma, it becomes 'a free-floating contagion, passing from uncomprehending witness to uncomprehending witness, dislocated from its historical origins—untethered to temporal or spatial coordinates' (Bond 2015: 49).

For LaCapra, such processes allow for an 'indiscriminate generalization of the category of survivor and the overall conflation of history or culture with trauma' (2014: xxxi). This universalization of trauma is engendered by the confusion of loss (which is historical) and absence (which is structural). While 'the historical past is the scene of losses that may be narrated', 'absence is not an event and does not imply tenses (past, present, or future)' (2014: 49). In other words, loss is the product of discrete historical events, resulting from the removal or destruction of a person, place, or thing. Absence, on the other hand, refers to the lack of foundations (be they referential, ideological, theological, or some other structural component) that *have never existed*. Put slightly differently:

> individuals and groups ... face particular losses in distinct ways, and those losses cannot be adequately addressed when they are enveloped in an overly generalized discourse of absence, including the absence of ultimate metaphysical foundations. Conversely, absence at a 'foundational' level cannot be simply derived from particular historical losses, however much it may be suggested or its recognition prompted by their magnitude and the intensity of one's response to them.
>
> (LaCapra 2014: 45–46)

LaCapra goes on to suggest that conflating these two categories of privation can have significant ethical and political consequences. For him, absence converted into loss can manifest as a 'misplaced nostalgia' (2014: 46) that drives a quest for a utopian politics, divorced from the conditions of the present reality. By contrast, when loss is mistaken for absence, a form of 'endless melancholy' (2014: 46) can arise, frustrating any possibility of productive mourning or working-through.

At stake here is what LaCapra identifies as 'the dubious appropriation of the status of victim through vicarious or surrogate victimage' (2014: 71), resulting from an overidentification with the suffering of another person or group. As he notes, while '[e]veryone is subject to structural trauma', 'with respect to historical trauma and its representation, the distinction between victims, perpetrators, and bystanders is crucial' (2014: 79). As we saw in Chapter 1, acknowledging the difference between these categories is an important step in resisting 'the indiscriminate generalization of historical trauma into the idea of a wound culture or the notion that everyone is somehow a victim (or, for that matter, a survivor)' (2014: 77). However, LaCapra's concern is that the slippage between structural and historical trauma has the additional effect of weakening the distinction between victim, perpetrator, bystander, and witness. He recommends that we focus on fostering a *virtual* rather than *vicarious* relationship to the trauma of others. Such a relationship would not preclude the development of ethical forms of empathy and solidarity for victims and survivors, but would refute any kind of appropriation of their suffering.

To this end, LaCapra argues that 'the attentive secondary witness' should open themselves to the experience of 'empathic unsettlement', which 'involves a kind of virtual experience through which one puts oneself in the other's position while recognizing the difference of that position, and hence not taking the other's place' (2014: 78). Empathic unsettlement raises

> the problem of how to address traumatic events involving victimization, including the problem of composing narratives that neither confuse one's own voice or position with the victim's nor seek facile uplift, harmonization, or closure, but allow the unsettlement they address to affect the narrative's own movement in terms of both acting out and working through.
> (2014: 78)

The idea of empathic unsettlement has implications for many types of secondary witnesses, including therapists, cultural practitioners, and trauma theorists, all of whom seek to find a way through the narrative void that Caruth and others have identified as a primary effect of trauma. LaCapra sees cultural narratives, such as Toni Morrison's *Beloved* (1987), playing a crucial role in the development of empathic unsettlement, noting that the imaginative freedom afforded to fiction writers can produce 'thought-provoking, at times disconcerting' readings of 'events, experiences, and memory' that allow readers to approach historical suffering from a sympathetic, yet reflexive, distance. However, he sounds a cautionary note about the dangers of uncritical interpretative processes through which 'one who was not there comes (or is moved) to believe that he or she was there and presents fiction as if it were testimony or historical memoir' (LaCapra 2004: 132).

TRANSGENERATIONAL TRAUMA

LaCapra's discussion of the difference between virtual and vicarious experience raises the thorny question of how trauma can be transmitted from one person to another. This issue has preoccupied cultural trauma theorists for several decades now. Felman and Laub extend the Freudian notion of transference to argue that it is not only clinicians who may undergo secondary traumatization, but also students learning of traumatic experiences, viewers or readers of trauma narratives, and lay people listening to an account of traumatization. Meanwhile, as noted above, Caruth's work heightens the potential for vicarious traumatization even further by suggesting that trauma may be carried *textually* from person to person. Such contentions have attracted notable critiques (in the work of Ruth Leys (2000) and Amy Hungerford (2003) among others), which argue that this position is too literal and unrealistically overstates the potential for endless traumatization. However, there is no doubt that these interventions have radically expanded the category of secondary witnessing.

In recent years, a number of theorists have begun to nuance and develop the notion of transference, analysing its transgenerational reach and examining the changing technologies that might facilitate vicarious traumatization. One of the earliest contributions to the field was Marianne Hirsch's seminal work on 'postmemory', first introduced in an article in *Discourse* (1992) and subsequently developed in *Family Frames: Photography, Narrative, and Postmemory* (1997). Hirsch begins her article with an account of her childhood experience as an immigrant in Rhode Island. She recounts visiting her neighbours and landlords, the Jakubowiczes, with her parents. The Jakubowiczes were Holocaust survivors, and Hirsch vividly describes her fascination with the 'few photos framed on a small, round living room table' (1992: 4) in their apartment. As a girl, Hirsch found 'something distinctly discomforting about them', which made her 'both want to keep staring and to look away, to get away from them' (1992: 4). These photographs, which depicted the entire Jakubowicz family before the Holocaust, seemed to be 'hovering on the edge between life and death' (1992: 4). Hirsch recalls how, in years to come, she would experience a similar sensation looking at images of her own family, particularly those of her husband's aunt Frieda, also a concentration camp survivor. For Hirsch, these pictures represent 'the timeless presence of the past', begging 'for a narrative, for a listener, for a survivor's tale' (1992: 5). Drawing on Roland Barthes's and Susan Sontag's work on photography, Hirsch explores the dual temporality of such images, which seem at once to portend death in the future and freeze the subject in the past.

Hirsch argues that images linked to the Holocaust, whether explicitly or implicitly:

> are uniquely able to bring out this particular capacity of the photograph to hover between life and death, to capture only that which no longer exists, to suggest both the desire or the necessity and, at the same time, the difficulty or the impossibility, of mourning in the face of massive public trauma
>
> (1992: 6–7).

In the two photographs of the Jakubowiczes and Frieda, neither of which depicts the Holocaust overtly, 'the horror of looking is not necessarily *in* the image but in the story we provide to fill in what is left out of the image' (1992: 7). Hirsch finds a correlate to these images in Spiegelman's graphic novel *Maus II* (1991), the second instalment of his account of his parents' experiences in Auschwitz. Hirsch argues that the photographic depiction of Spiegelman's brother Richlieu (who did not survive the Holocaust) and his father Vladek, which augment the comic strip,

> connect the two levels of the text, past and present, the story of the father and the story of the son, because these family photographs are documents of both memory (the survivor's) and of ... post-memory (that of the child of the survivor whose life is dominated by memories of what preceded his/her birth).
>
> (1992: 8)

As Hirsch goes on to explain in her later work, '[p]ostmemory describes the relationship of the second generation to powerful, often traumatic, experiences that preceded their births but that were nevertheless transmitted to them so deeply as to seem to constitute memories in their own right' (2008: 1). It is distinguished from memory by 'generational distance' and from history by 'deep personal connection' (1997: 22).

For Hirsch, Spiegelman's *Maus* provides an exemplary representation of postmemory because it focuses on the transgenerational legacies of the Holocaust, foregrounding the genocide's effects on the survivor, Vladek, and Spiegelman's fictional alter ego Artie, who was born in America. Switching between different timeframes, *Maus* tells the story of the family's experiences during the war alongside Artie's attempts to coax Vladek's testimony from him and record it, in mediated form, in his own graphic novel. As Hirsch notes, *Maus* is a 'paradigmatic' postmemory text because it is 'a familial story, collaboratively constructed by father and son', which details how the Spiegelmans' 'family interactions are inflected by a history that refuses to remain in the background or outside the text':

> Their story is told, drawn, by their son who was born after the war but whose life was decisively determined by this familial and cultural memory. Art Spiegelman's memory is delayed, indirect, secondary, it is a postmemory of the Holocaust mediated by the father-survivor but determinative for the son.
>
> (1997: 13)

Hirsch's theory of postmemory thus suggests that the imprint of trauma can be passed down through generations as the children of survivors inherit memories of catastrophic events they did not themselves live through. While the first generation may remain immediately traumatized by their experiences, for their children the traces of trauma inhere in narratives, photographs, and other objectified or affective forms, which may well, paradoxically, include silences and absences. The task of 'the generation of postmemory', then, is precisely to *claim* this experience and to find some way of assimilating it into their own life-story. Hirsch's thesis, expanded in *The Generation of Postmemory: Writing and Visual Culture after the Holocaust* (2012), is that, for postgeneration artists and writers such as Spiegelman, W. G. Sebald, Eva Hoffman, Tatana Kellner, Lorie Novak, and David Levinthal, cultural representations provide a powerful way of acknowledging this traumatic legacy.

Unlike Caruth's account of trauma, which emphasizes the directness of traumatic recall, postmemory is a heavily mediated form of remembrance. However, recent research in epigenetics has suggested that trauma may travel across generations in an altogether more literal way. While epigenetics remains a nascent and controversial field, a number of studies have argued that trauma can leave a chemical mark on a person's genes, which is then passed down to the following generation. Although this trace does not cause any direct genetic mutation, supporters of this theory argue that it can alter 'the mechanism by which the gene is converted into functioning proteins, or expressed' (Carey 2018), affecting the health of the next generation in unexpected ways. In 2018, for example, a study of American Civil War prisoners found that male children of abused detainees were around ten per cent more likely to die at an early age than their peers. The authors attributed these premature deaths to epigenetic changes linked to the trauma of their fathers' incarceration (Carey 2018). Similar findings have been reported in foetal survivors of the Dutch Hunger Winter of 1944–1945, during which 20,000 people died of starvation after the Nazis blocked food supplies into the Netherlands. A 2013 investigation led by L. H. Lumey and Bas Heijmans found that adults who were in utero during the famine 'ended up a few pounds heavier than average. In middle age, they had higher levels of triglycerides and LDL cholesterol. They also experienced higher rates of such conditions as obesity, diabetes and schizophrenia' (Zimmer 2018). Lumley and Heijmans attributed such anomalies to the fact that the experience of the famine may have permanently affected particular genes in vulnerable foetuses, which have remained fundamentally altered ever since (Tobi *et al.* 2018). Similar claims have also been advanced about the children of Holocaust and 9/11 survivors and victims of poverty.

As Benedict Carey notes, '[i]f these studies hold up, they would suggest that we inherit some trace of our parents' and even grandparents' experience, particularly their suffering, which in turn modifies our own day-to-day health—and perhaps our children's, too' (2018). However, these studies continue to attract a large number of detractors, and the scientific community has not come to any consensus about the viability of such claims. As Carey comments:

> The idea that we carry some biological trace of our ancestors' pain has a strong emotional appeal. It resonates with the feelings that arise when one views images of famine, war or slavery. And it seems to buttress psychodynamic narratives about trauma, and how its legacy can reverberate through families and down the ages. But for now, and for many scientists, the research in epigenetics falls well short of demonstrating that past human cruelties affect our physiology today, in any predictable or consistent way.
>
> (2018)

FANTASIES OF WITNESSING

Whether or not one is convinced by the idea that traumatic experiences may be transmitted culturally or biologically from one generation to the next, it is important to note that both Hirsch's original conception of postmemory and recent work in epigenetics maintain a direct link between the immediate victim or survivor and the inheritor of their trauma. However, in recent years, Hirsch has expanded her discussion to include what she describes as 'affiliative' rather than 'familial' postmemory. In Hoffman's terms, Hirsch has broadened her focus beyond 'the literal second generation in particular' to 'the post-generation as a whole' (2004: 187). Her later work suggests that postmemory is not, in fact, 'limited to the intimate embodied space of the family', and may 'extend to more distant, adoptive witnesses or affiliative contemporaries' (M. Hirsch 2012: 6).

Other accounts of secondary traumatization have also dispensed with the ties of family relationships, suggesting that mass mediation may make it possible for trauma to be transmitted *prosthetically* between people with no lived relation to the originary event. The notion of 'prosthetic memory' has its origins in the work of Alison Landsberg, who argues that 'modernity makes possible and necessary a new form of public cultural memory', which 'emerges at the interface of a person and a historical narrative about the past, at an experiential site such as a movie theater or a museum' (2004: 2). Confronted with a story that may have no direct connection to their own lived experience, the witness undergoes a 'moment of contact' with a mediated memory that they encounter in a commodified form, such as a film, a novel, or an exhibition. At this moment, 'an experience occurs through which the person sutures himself or herself into a larger history' (2004: 4). The witness

> does not simply apprehend a historical narrative but takes on a more personal, deeply felt memory of a past event through which he or she did not live. The resulting prosthetic memory has the ability to shape that person's subjectivity and politics.
>
> (2004: 2)

While this kind of recognition seems intrinsic to various forms of literary reading, Landsberg is particularly interested in the experience of reading about, or listening to, narratives of trauma. Her account of prosthetic memory embraces a number of historical experiences: from the lives of African Americans after slavery, through early-twentieth-century US immigration, to Jewish suffering during the Holocaust. She argues that each of these cases demonstrates that 'modernity's ruptures do not belong exclusively to a particular group; that is, memories of the Holocaust do not belong only to Jews, nor do memories of slavery belong solely to African Americans' (2004: 2). Rather, through the technologies of mass culture, 'it becomes possible for these memories to be acquired by anyone, regardless of skin color, ethnic background, or biology' (2004: 2). The production and transmission of prosthetic memory relies on the ability of mass media representations to construct '*transferential spaces* in the Freudian sense' (2004: 23) in which 'people may have an experience of events through which they did not live' (2004: 24). Examining cultural artefacts including Cecil B. DeMille's film *The Road to Yesterday* (1925), Octavia Butler's novel

Kindred (1979), Spiegelman's *Maus,* and Steven Spielberg's film *Schindler's List* (1993), Landsberg explores how 'the turn to mass culture—to movies, experiential museums, television shows, and so forth—has made what was once considered a group's private memory available to a much broader public' (2004: 11).

Landsberg does not strictly argue that prosthetic memories are traumatizing. However, the idea of mass-mediated trauma (or rather, of traumatization via exposure to media accounts) gained popularity in the aftermath of the terrorist attacks of 11 September 2001. A global event, watched live by an estimated two billion people (Panero 2014), 9/11 was, from the start, a mass-mediated atrocity. As the vast majority of those who witnessed the event did so on television, it is perhaps unsurprising that mental health professionals soon suggested that exposure to media footage could lead to traumatization. Indeed, in the immediate aftermath of the attacks, the American Psychological Association issued a press release advising members of the public to articulate their concerns to 'trained officials throughout the country' and '[l]imit exposure to media coverage' (American Psychological Association 2001). The idea that experiencing 9/11 vicariously through television footage could lead to traumatization was subsequently given weight by the media and cultural trauma theorists. The possibility of media trauma dramatically expanded the potential scale of traumatization, from those who directly experienced or witnessed the attacks in New York and Washington DC to a global audience of television viewers. As the *New York Times* later declared, 9/11 thus became a 'trauma that rippled outward' (Haberman 2009).

In her book *Trauma Culture: The Politics of Terror and Loss in Media and Literature* (2005), literary scholar E. Ann Kaplan suggests that, in an age of mass communication, 'most people encounter trauma through the media' (2005: 2). Kaplan argues that, for this very reason, the attacks of 11 September reveal 'the difficulty of fully distinguishing trauma from vicarious trauma' (2005: 2). This is a very important point, which highlights some of the conceptual issues associated with the idea of media trauma. As Kaplan notes, when faced with a mass-mediated catastrophe such as 9/11, 'it is necessary to distinguish the different positions and contexts of encounters with trauma' (2005: 2):

> At the one extreme there is the direct trauma victim while at the other we find a person geographically far away, having no personal connection to the victim. In between are a series of positions: for example, there's the relative to trauma victims or the position of workers coming in after a catastrophe, those who encounter trauma via the accounts they hear, or clinicians who may be vicariously traumatized.
>
> (2005: 2)

These distinctions may seem blindingly obvious; however, the 'prosthetic' technologies of contemporary trauma culture appear to blur the boundaries between immediate experience and secondary witnessing. This complicates the neat spectrum of traumatization that Kaplan outlines above and can lead to the formation of what Gary Weissman describes as 'fantasies of witnessing' (2004).

Weissman's work emerges from his interest in 'post-war efforts to experience the Holocaust' (2004). He argues that Holocaust memoirs (such as Elie Wiesel's *Night* (1960)), museums (such as the United States Holocaust Memorial Museum), and films (such as *Schindler's List*) can, wittingly or unwittingly, encourage their audiences to assume an intimate relationship to traumas with which they have no immediate connection. As Weissman explains:

> the term *nonwitness* stresses that we who were not there did not witness the Holocaust, and that the experience of listening to, reading or viewing witness testimony is substantially unlike the experience of victimization. We can read books or watch films on the Holocaust, listen to Holocaust survivors, visit Holocaust museums, take trips to Holocaust memorial sites in Europe, research and write about the Holocaust, look at photographs of the victims, and so forth, but in none of these cases are we witnessing the actual events of the Holocaust. Rather, we are experiencing representations of the Holocaust, all of them created or preserved in its aftermath.
>
> (2004: 20)

The danger is that, by encouraging viewers or visitors to overidentify with historical suffering, the mediated cultural products of what the American political scientist Norman Finkelstein controversially calls 'the Holocaust industry' (2000) blur the line between the experiences of non-witnesses and those of actual victims and survivors.

In the case of *Schindler's List*, Weissman contends that the hyper-realist aesthetic of the film, which is the signature characteristic of Spielberg's direction, confuses fantasy and historical reality in such a way that it encourages viewers to feel as if they were actually 'there'. As one reviewer (cited by Weissman) notes of a key scene:

> About an hour into the film, Spielberg stages the liquidation of the Krakow ghetto, and in this turbulent and almost unbearably vivid fifteen-minute sequence the Holocaust, fifty years removed from our contemporary consciousness, suddenly becomes overwhelmingly immediate, undeniable
>
> (Rafferty 1993: 130).

Scenes such as this one lead Weissman to describe *Schindler's List* as 'the most aggressive attempt to date to re-create the Holocaust as a spectacle that can be witnessed and mourned' (1995: 306). Viewers of *Schindler's List* may approach the film with the genuine intention of understanding more about the genocide by truly engaging with its horror. However, Weissman contends, Spielberg's obsessive verisimilitude furthers the promise that '[i]n watching *Schindler's List*, nonwitnesses can witness for themselves (re-created) events that they have only read or heard about; furthermore, in recognizing these events, they can validate their own knowingness as Holocaust initiates' (2004: 149).

Herein lies the crux of the ethical compromise that accompanies fantasies of witnessing. While Weissman acknowledges that some forms of secondary witnessing 'grant the children of survivors a "position of privilege" closer, as it were, to the Holocaust', he is concerned that films like *Schindler's List* enable non-witnesses 'to convince themselves and others that they too occupy a privileged position in relation to the event' (2004: 21). This can push the viewer from empathizing with onscreen suffering to overidentifying with the victims of trauma, losing sight of their own distance from the events, and mistaking the filmic representation for the historical reality of the Holocaust. The process of engaging with the Holocaust can thus become a solipsistic exercise in self-affirmation, as Weissman explains:

> For nonwitnesses, one's own place in the hierarchy of suffering has much to do with one's professed ability to 'feel the horror'. One's intellect and moral fiber are measured by the degree that one has come ... to 'endure the psychic imprint of the trauma'. Here, 'trauma' becomes a sign of one's authentic relationship to the Holocaust: if one has *really* faced the Holocaust, felt its horror and remembered its victims, one must be 'traumatized' by the experience.
>
> (2004: 21)

At its worst, such a position can be appropriative if not highly exploitative.

The problems that attend such fantasies of witnessing are further explored by Hungerford. In *The Holocaust of Texts: Genocide, Literature, and Personification* (2003), she critiques the tendency to view historical testimonies and fictions as if the texts themselves were embodiments of lived experience. Hungerford argues that it has become commonplace to personify texts, a habit that she traces to the legal, political, and cultural discourses about genocide that circulated in the aftermath of the Second World War. The act of personification, she contends, 'represents a set of strategies by which something ordinarily thought to be particular to conscious (or, in some cases, merely living) beings comes to be assigned to a text' (2003: 17). This may happen in a number of different ways: it might mean, for example, 'that the text is imagined as having a body, as being aware of its own mortality, as having the capacity to have or embody experience, or as being the highest moral value relative to other objects in the world' (2003: 17).

Hungerford's study examines different forms of personification in a broad range of postwar literature, including Spiegelman's *Maus*, Ray Bradbury's *Fahrenheit 451* (1953), the poetry of Sylvia Plath, and Binjamin Wilkormirski's infamous fake Holocaust memoir *Fragments* (1996). However, she also argues that

> Postwar criticism and literary theory has shared this tendency to imagine the literary text as if it bore significant characteristics of persons, despite the effort made in two of the most powerful twentieth-century

critical movements, New Criticism and deconstruction, to limit and critique the relationship between persons and texts.

(2003: 4)

Among the thinkers whom Hungerford indicts for failing to differentiate between texts and lives are Felman and Caruth, as well as other theorists such as Jacqueline Rose, Paul de Man, and Jacques Derrida. For Hungerford, 'the collapse of persons and representations' (2003: 78) that takes place in certain examples of cultural trauma theory perpetuates the issue of vicarious witnessing by reinforcing 'the fantasy of the personified text':

the fantasy that we can really have another person's experience, that we can be someone else, that we can somehow possess a culture that we do not practice, elides the gap that imagination—preferable ... to identification—must fill. We must find ourselves not in the other (or the other in ourselves) but the other as we can know them without being them.

(2003: 157)

Such assumptions have both literary-critical and political ramifications. First, Hungerford argues, the conflation of texts and persons impoverishes our idea of art by privileging life over imagination. Second, it impoverishes our ideas of persons 'since it renders the fact of embodiment irrelevant, when embodiment is exactly what situates us in history and makes us vulnerable to oppression' (2003: 21).

Hungerford is ultimately concerned about the ethical implications of such developments. She explains that 'social justice requires us to be able to recognize the otherness of other persons, an otherness that is belied by an understanding of literature based on the mechanisms of identification' (2003: 21). The danger is that, 'if we imagine that we can actually have another's experience by reading about it, it may short-circuit more substantive efforts at understanding and entering into relationship with those who are culturally or otherwise unlike us' (2003: 21). In Weissman's terms, there is thus the very real possibility that the fantasy of witnessing produced by mediated forms of engagement may replace a more reflexive relationship to traumatic histories. Or, in LaCapra's formulation, in personifying works of literature, we run the risk of overidentifying with the suffering of others and precluding the emergence of empathic unsettlement.

Faced with these problems, Efraim Sicher (2000: 67) argues that cultural trauma theory has been insufficiently attentive to the conflation of primary and secondary forms of witnessing in contemporary trauma culture. He indicts theories of vicarious witnessing for what he considers to be an insufficient differentiation between witnesses, descendants, and imaginary identifications with victims. To be fair, these issues affect the work of the critics we have considered to varying extents. As we have seen, Kaplan remains attentive to a spectrum of traumatic experience, which stretches from direct exposure to the catalysing event to the vicarious witnessing of media footage. Hirsch, too, acknowledges that 'lines of relation and identification need to be theorized more closely' to find out how 'identification can resist appropriation and incorporation, resist annihilating the difference between self and other, the otherness of the other' (2001: 11). However, Landsberg reaches the contentious conclusion that '[a]ny distinction between "real" memories and prosthetic memories—memories that might be technologically disseminated as commodities by the mass media and worn by their consumers—might ultimately be unimportant' (2004: 45).

These tensions point to a wider debate in cultural trauma theory, which concerns the relationship between individual and collective trauma. As the final section of this chapter demonstrates, while some theorists assume that trauma affects communities in basically the same way as it does individuals, others have questioned the unproblematic extension of clinically derived terms to larger entities and suggested that we think of collective or cultural trauma as a social construction.

INDIVIDUAL AND COLLECTIVE TRAUMA

As we saw in Chapter 1, in *Moses and Monotheism* (1939; see 2010b) Freud conceptualized collective trauma in the image of an individual neurosis. *Moses and Monotheism* was not the first text in which he draws a parallel between individual and collective pathologies. In *Totem and Taboo* (1912), for example, Freud argues that 'religious phenomena are to be understood only on the model of the neurotic symptoms of the individual … as a return of long forgotten important happenings in the primaeval history of the human family' (2010b: 94). These claims are repeated and developed in his final work. Seeking a 'deeper knowledge of the historical and psychological conditions of [the] origin [of the religion]' (2010b: 96), Freud suggests that the roots of modern Judaism lie in a history that is characterized by '*duality*' (2010b: 84) and rupture.

Freud begins his study by arguing that the Moses who led the Jews out of Egypt would not have been the son of Jewish slaves, as scripture suggests, but an Egyptian nobleman of high birth. From this claim it follows that the monotheistic tradition to which Moses and his followers subscribed would not have been that of the Hebrew god Jahve (or Yahweh), but Aton, an ancient Egyptian deity. Drawing on the work of the historian Ernst Sellin, Freud goes on to argue that, having freed the Jews and led the Exodus out of Egypt, the Egyptian Moses 'met a violent end in a rebellion of his stubborn and refractory people. The religion he had instituted was at the same time abandoned' (2010b: 59). Some two generations after his murder, in this story, Moses's followers combined with worshippers of Jahve who had settled at Qadēs, an oasis in the desert. It was through the union of these tribes that the people of Israel were born; the stories of Moses and Jahve were integrated into a new doctrine, founded by a man who was also named Moses.

Freud argues that the memory of the first Moses was subsequently displaced by that of the second Moses. As their stories were conflated, the two Moses were transposed into a single figure who led the Jews out of Israel *and* founded a new religion in the oasis. Freud sees this rewriting of history as a process of traumatic erasure, motivated by collective regret over the murder of the first Moses, which was thereafter forgotten. Over time, however, the characteristics of Jahve, who was now the sole god of the Israelites, increasingly started to resemble those of 'the old God of Moses, Aton' (2010b: 103). Freud describes the process through which long-buried aspects of the past began to possess the present as an 'incubation period' akin to the 'grave psychical and motor symptoms' that a patient might suffer following a railway accident (2010b: 109). He notes that, 'in spite of the fundamental difference in the two cases, the problem of the traumatic neuroses and that of Jewish

Monotheism … there is a correspondence in one point. It is the feature which one might term *latency*' (2010b: 109–10).

In making this analogy, Freud invites his reader to 'assume that in the history of the human species something happened similar to the events in the life of the individual' (2010b: 129). He concludes that 'the concordance between the individual and the mass is … almost complete. The masses, too, retain an impression of the past in unconscious memory traces' (2010b: 151). According to this logic, '[i]f we accept the continued existence of such memory-traces in our archaic inheritance then we have bridged the gap between individual and mass psychology, and can treat people as we do the individual neurotic' (2010b: 160). As may be apparent, Freud's account of *Moses and Monotheism* contains some odd slippages, which make a number of its claims hard to substantiate. As many critics have pointed out, the narrative on which Freud depends for his explanation of Jewish history is fundamentally a product of his own interpretation and departs from established historical and theological accounts. Moreover, Freud's analysis slips rapidly from the particular origins of modern Judaism to a discussion of human history in general, revising many elements of his earlier works and rehearsing his major psychoanalytic findings. The text thus contains several departures of its own, which always presage a return to the immediate context of writing. It is these moments of rupture—or rather, as she sees them, of latency—that impel Caruth's interest in the work.

Caruth is particularly fascinated by two particular passages in *Moses and Monotheism.* The first connects the murder of Moses to an earlier murder in the history of mankind, 'the murder of the primal father by his rebellious sons, which occurred in primeval history' (1996: 18). Freud suggests that, after a period of latency, the second murder, that of Moses, forms an unconscious recognition of the first, and is itself recreated in the death of Christ, which St Paul interprets as an atonement for an original sin (Freud 2010b: 137–45). In this reading, Christ symbolically becomes 'the resurrected Moses and the returned primaeval father of the primitive horde as well' (2010b: 144–45). For Caruth, this passage marks the arrival of the Jewish people 'within a history no longer simply their own', revealing how 'the inscription of Jews in history is always bound to the history of the Christians' (1996: 18). The central insight of

Moses and Monotheism, therefore, is that 'history, like trauma, is never simply one's own, that history is precisely the way we are implicated in each other's traumas' (1996: 24).

This understanding is borne out by a second example. Caruth is fascinated by the structure of Freud's text, and in particular by how the earlier sections of the book—Parts I and II, which were published in 1937, before he left Austria—are interrupted by the two prefaces to Part III, published after Freud's exile in London, and largely repeated in a section called 'Summary and Recapitulation'. As Caruth notes, '[t]he structure and history of the book, in its traumatic form of repression and repetitive reappearance, thus mark it as the very bearer of a historical truth' (1996: 20). In this reading, the book becomes the site of

> a trauma that ... appears to be historically marked by the events that, Freud says, divide the book into two halves: first, the infiltration of Nazism into Austria, causing Freud to withhold or repress the third part, and then the invasion of Austria by Germany, causing Freud to leave and ultimately to bring the third part to light.
>
> (1996: 20)

For Caruth, this act of literal displacement resembles the latency of trauma; it is analogous to 'the traumatic event [that] is not experienced as it occurs', but that 'is fully evident only in connection with another place, and in another time' (1995a: 8). Here, Freud's text and the history contained within it stand in for the traumatic event, becoming accessible only after his departure for the UK.

Moses and Monotheism exposes the communal dimensions of trauma in two different ways. By construing the murder of Moses as restaging the killing of the primeval father and foreshadowing the crucifixion of Christ, Caruth argues, Freud reveals that traumatic pasts are inherently entangled with one another. Then, by highlighting the period of latency that attended the publication of the third part of his text, Freud demonstrates how the act of 'departure within trauma ... is also a means of passing out of the isolation imposed by the event' (Caruth 1995a: 10–11). In seeking a public audience for his story, Freud showed that 'the history of a trauma ... can only take place through the listening of another' (Caruth 1995a:

11). For Caruth, the text thus becomes symptomatic 'not only [of] individual isolation but [of] a wider historical isolation that, in our time, is communicated on the level of our cultures' (1995a: 11). This leads her to conclude that, '[i]n a catastrophic age … trauma itself may provide the very link between cultures' (1995a: 11).

As Richard Crownshaw notes, in drawing wider significance from Freud's work, Caruth's account represents a 'transposition of individual psychoanalytical states onto cultural scenarios' (2010: 22). However, a number of critics have found this straightforward mapping of psychological dynamics onto collective social entities too unempirical, and have sought to nuance this model of collective trauma. Writing in Caruth's edited volume *Trauma: Explorations in Memory*, Erikson, a sociologist, offers a slightly different model of the relationship between trauma and community. Erikson's analysis draws on his experience of disasters in the US and Canada, including the 1972 Buffalo Creek flood and the deadly nuclear accident at Three Mile Island in 1979. Like Freud and Caruth, Erikson concedes that, 'when the community is profoundly affected, one can speak of a damaged social organism in almost the same way that one would speak of a damaged body' (1995: 188). However, he argues, 'one can think about traumatized communities as something distinct from traumatized persons' (1995: 185).

Erikson's experience with traumatized groups lends a specificity to his discussion that is lacking in Caruth's account of transcultural trauma. His research suggests that 'communal trauma can take two forms, either alone or in combination: damage to the tissues that hold human groups intact, and the creation of social climates, communal moods, that come to dominate a group's spirit' (1995: 190). As a result of these two trends, trauma can build community by giving victims 'a feeling that they have been set apart and made special' (1995: 186). In this sense, individual victims (of even unrelated traumas) may come together to form a collective. However, rather than suggesting that, by dint of this finding, traumatized collectives (transhistorically and universally) function like traumatized individuals, Erikson makes a welcome distinction between individual and collective trauma. By *individual trauma*, he explains, he means 'a blow to the psyche that breaks through one's defences so suddenly and with such brutal force that one cannot react to it effectively' (1976: 153). By *collective trauma*, he refers to 'a blow to the basic tissues of social life that damages the bonds attaching people together and impairs the prevailing sense of community' (1976: 154). In other words, Erikson distinguishes here between the *psychological* nature of individual trauma and the *social* nature of collective trauma.

This crucial distinction has characterized subsequent work on collective trauma. Neal argues that, while '[t]he concept of trauma is applied primarily to extraordinary experiences in the personal lives of individuals', it 'may also be applied collectively to the experiences of an entire group of people. Here conditions of trauma grow out of an injury, a wound, or an assault on social life as it is known and understood' (2005: 3–4). He is particularly interested in the relationship between American national trauma (examples of which include the assassination of Abraham Lincoln, the Great Depression, the attack on Pearl Harbor, and 9/11) and personal identity. For Neal, 'national trauma differs from a personal trauma in that it is shared with others' (2005: 4). Yet, 'national traumas have meaning for individuals through the creation of links between personal thought and action and the historical dimensions of their time and place' (2005: 16). The magnitude of a national trauma is such that 'it commands the attention of all major subgroups of the population. Even those who are usually apathetic and indifferent to national affairs are drawn into the public arena of discussion and debate' (2005: 12).

While Neal is right to argue that national traumas have political ramifications, his account is slow to recognize how they are politically constructed. In his discussion of 11 September 2001 (which he describes as a 'national trauma of intense proportions' (2005: 179)), for example, Neal acknowledges the divisive legacies of 9/11, including the wars in Afghanistan and Iraq, the indefinite detention of terror suspects in Guantánamo and elsewhere, and the restriction of civil liberties at home. However, he does not examine how the framing of the attacks *as* a national trauma may have paved the way for the Bush administration to pursue its retributive policies (Edkins 2003; Pease 2009; Bond 2015). Richard Clarke, the national coordinator for security and counterterrorism under Presidents Bill Clinton and George W. Bush, describes this ploy as 'the White House 9/11 trauma defense', through which the government sought to absolve itself of responsibility for its actions 'on the grounds that 9/11 was traumatic' (2009). As Walter Davis expands,

> The response of the Bush Administration to the trauma of 9/11 presents a particularly revealing, if extreme, example of the ... dominant response to trauma. First, a proclamation of our innocence and victimhood. Second, a massive act of projective evacuation—the war in Iraq—as the only way to restore our identity.
>
> (2009: 139)

The upshot of this was that '[a]ny chance that 9/11 might have brought about painful reflections on America and its actions in the world are [sic] thereby banished' (2009: 139–40).

As James Trimarco and Molly Hurley Depret reflect, the American media were complicit in this framing of 9/11. In the immediate aftermath of the attacks, 'most newspapers and television stations labeled the event a national trauma without hesitation or explanation' (2005: 30). Subsequently, '[m]uch of what has been written about the attacks assumes that the attacks formed a "wound" on the collective psyche of *all* Americans, causing trauma and requiring particular sorts of healing' (2005: 30). On the one hand, then, describing an event such as 9/11 as a national trauma elides the degree to which that very label might be both ideologically expedient and politically constructed. On the other hand, the very idea of a national trauma can homogenize different kinds of response and obscure important differences in the perceptions of groups and individuals. If these dangers are not acknowledged, Susannah Radstone writes, accounts of collective trauma risk 'hardening into literality what might better be regarded as a series of compelling metaphors—the "traumatisation" of a nation, for instance, or the "healing" of a culture' (2005: 44).

Alert to such nuances, Eyerman and Alexander highlight the *constructed* nature of public narratives surrounding trauma. As Eyerman comments, 'a national trauma must be understood, explained, and made coherent through public reflection and discourse. Here mass media and their representations play a decisive role' (2004: 61). Taking this one step further, he argues, '[a]llowing for the centrality of mediation and imaginative reconstruction, one should perhaps not speak of traumatic events, but rather of traumatic effects ... While trauma necessarily refers to something experienced in psychological accounts, calling this experience *traumatic* requires interpretation' (2004: 62). Alexander expands, '[c]ollective traumas are reflections neither of individual suffering nor actual events, but symbolic renderings that reconstruct and imagine them' (2012: 4). Eyerman and Alexander here point to the fact that, in order to be regarded as collective or national traumas, events have to be constructed as such in the public sphere. Only when reinforced in mainstream cultural, political, and media discourses 'is traumatic status attributed to an event' (Alexander 2004: 10). Thus, Alexander concludes, '[e]vents are not inherently traumatic. Trauma is a socially mediated attribution' (2004: 8). During the 'process of trauma creation' (2004: 1), various social agents (broadcasters, journalists, politicians, artists, etc.) shape the public narratives surrounding an event until it has been naturalized as traumatic.

In order to emphasize this process of mediation, Eyerman and Alexander prefer the term 'cultural trauma' to 'collective' or 'national' trauma. As Neil Smelser argues, cultural trauma describes

> a memory accepted and publicly given credence by a relevant membership group and evoking an event or situation which is a) laden with negative affect, b) represented as indelible, and c) regarded as threatening a society's existence or violating one or more of its fundamental cultural presuppositions.
>
> (2004: 44)

Eyerman, Alexander, and Smelser are by no means suggesting that the social impact of cultural trauma is in any way artificial or unreal. On the contrary, Alexander clarifies that cultural trauma occurs 'when members of a collectivity feel they have been subjected to a horrendous event that leaves indelible marks on their group consciousness' (2004: 1). Rather, they are eager to emphasize the fact that collective consciousness does not function in the same way as an individual psyche, and so, in order to register as traumatic at a social level, an event must be recurrently designated as such. As Alexander points out, 'this is a matter of intense cultural and political work' (2012: 2), and '[t]he spiral of signification is mediated by institutional structures and uneven distributions of wealth and power' (2012: 4).

As this chapter has aimed to demonstrate, over the past thirty years the emergence of cultural trauma theory has led to a growing interest in forms of secondary or vicarious witnessing, transgenerational or prosthetic memory, and collective, national, or cultural traumas. Work in this area has increasingly focused on the ways that lived experience, and especially the experience of suffering and victimhood, is mediated by different forms of cultural production. These interventions have successively expanded and nuanced the frames through which trauma and its transmission can be understood. However, as the final chapter will explore, changing circumstances and ideas continue to challenge established understandings of trauma and push trauma studies in new and exciting directions.

4

THE FUTURE OF TRAUMA

This chapter focuses on a number of recent developments in the field of trauma theory, which has grown significantly since the early 1990s. It will not so much reflect on the past of trauma theory as consider its future. As such, this chapter is itself symptomatic of the current state of the field, since quite a few stocktaking efforts have recently been made by trauma scholars. Examples include three edited collections: *Contemporary Approaches in Literary Trauma Theory* (Balaev 2014), *The Future of Trauma Theory: Contemporary Literary and Cultural Criticism* (Buelens *et al.* 2014), and *The Future of Memory* (Crownshaw *et al.* 2010). Part of the last collection is specifically devoted to 'The Future of Trauma'. Another book that comes to mind in this context is Alan Gibbs's important monograph *Contemporary American Trauma Narratives* (2014). Like these four books, this chapter can be seen to reflect a certain unease about trauma theory becoming a field: a concern that a set of valuable and complex ideas and insights may be congealing into a rigid method or creed and thereby losing the capacity for self-reflection and the original investigative or ethical impulse. With the editors and author of these volumes, all of which are explicitly future-oriented, we share a determination to prevent this from happening. If trauma theory had seemed to be stagnating somewhat since its early burst of creative energy in the 1990s, we see various signs of renewal and continuing relevance.

This chapter consists of four sections, in each of which we will analyse one promising new trend that responds to established criticisms of various aspects of trauma theory. In the first section, we will discuss the emerging tendency to study trauma as a global rather than a European or Western phenomenon. In the second part, we will address recent attempts to move beyond normative trauma aesthetics, which would involve abandoning the popular notion that a modernist aesthetic of formal experimentation is uniquely suited to the task of bearing witness to trauma. The third section will look at the shift or broadening of focus from victim trauma to perpetrator trauma: the tendency to no longer limit one's inquiry to the experiences of victims but to also take on board those of perpetrators as well as other categories of people implicated in traumatic events or histories. In the fourth and final section, we will explore theorizations of pre-traumatic stress, a kind of before-the-fact version of PTSD that is seen by some critics as a defining condition of human beings in the current era.

DECOLONIZING TRAUMA

In *The Future of Memory,* Jane Kilby, one of the book's editors, states that, while the future of trauma theory is to a large extent unpredictable, 'for certain the question of globalization will dominate' (2010: 181). This prediction, made in 2010, is being borne out, as the last few years have seen the publication of a number of monographs, edited collections, and special journal issues that aim to move the field beyond its Eurocentric boundaries. Indeed, the tendency to regard trauma as a transcultural, transnational, or global phenomenon is one of the most pronounced trends in trauma scholarship of the last decade. While 'Western' traumas such as the Holocaust and 9/11 continue to attract a great deal of interest, cultural trauma research has lately begun to diversify. It now also includes a significant amount of work addressing other kinds of traumatic experiences, such as those associated with slavery, colonialism, apartheid, Partition, and the Stolen Generations, and there are a growing number of publications that adopt a cross-cultural comparative perspective.

The mental health profession's traditional blindness to the psychic suffering of people of colour is captured by a brief poem in the Jamaican American poet Claudia Rankine's *Citizen: An American Lyric* (2014), a collection that examines the experience of racism in the United States and the West more generally through vignettes of everyday discrimination and prejudice, and meditations on the violence, whether linguistic or physical, that has impacted the lives of Serena Williams, Zinedine Zidane, Mark Duggan, and other racially marked subjects. The poem in question recounts the first encounter between a mental health professional who 'specializes in trauma counseling' and a patient who unexpectedly turns up on her front doorstep after finding the side gate that leads to the back entrance, which the therapist normally uses for patients, locked (2014: 18). Having only spoken with them on the phone before, the therapist evidently assumed her new patient to be white, but he or she turns out to be black. In fact, she does not immediately recognize them as her patient but sees them as an intruder and trespasser, and reacts in anger and fear:

> When the door finally opens, the woman standing there yells, at the top of her lungs, Get away from my house! What are you doing in my yard?
>
> It's as if a wounded Doberman pinscher or a German shepherd has gained the power of speech.
>
> (2014: 18)

It is not until the unwelcome guest manages to tell her that they actually have an appointment that it dawns on her that this is in fact her new patient, and on realizing her mistake, she apologizes profusely:

> You have an appointment? she spits back. Then she pauses. Everything pauses. Oh, she says, followed by, oh, yes, that's right. I am sorry.
>
> I am so sorry, so, so sorry.
>
> (2014: 18)

This anecdote reads like an allegory of the insensitivity to racial and cultural difference characteristic of traditional trauma theory, an attitude that, it is implied, generates further trauma: after all, the person of colour on the receiving end of the trauma counsellor's rage is made to suffer a 'microaggression' as a result of being verbally assaulted and treated like dirt, and such experiences can foster traumatic responses as they accrue over time. As Stef Craps has shown in *Postcolonial Witnessing: Trauma Out of Bounds* (2013), the founding texts of cultural trauma theory have indeed tended to marginalize or ignore traumatic experiences of non-Western or minority groups. Despite the omnipresence of violence and suffering in the world, most attention within trauma theory has been devoted to events that took place in Europe or the United States. As is apparent from the work of Cathy Caruth, Shoshana Felman, Dori Laub, Geoffrey Hartman, and Dominick LaCapra, trauma theory as a field of cultural scholarship developed out of an engagement with Holocaust testimony, literature, and history. As we saw in Chapter 3, a further flurry of trauma-theoretical publications followed in the wake of the terrorist attacks of 9/11. It has been argued that this rather one-sided focus on key Western trauma sites is at odds with trauma theory's self-proclaimed ethical aspirations, and that a broadening of focus is called for if the field is to have any hope of redeeming its promise of promoting cross-cultural solidarity (Craps 2013). The pertinence of this postcolonial critique would appear to be borne out by the fact that Caruth addresses it in the afterword to the 2016 twentieth-anniversary edition of *Unclaimed Experience*, in which she elaborates on her reading, in the introduction to the book, of the Italian Renaissance poet Torquato Tasso's story of Tancred and Clorinda as mediated by Sigmund Freud.

The expansion of the usual Eurocentric focus of trauma theory that we have witnessed over the last few years has gone hand in hand with a critical questioning of the supposed universal validity of Western definitions of trauma and recovery. While trauma tends to be thought of as a timeless, acultural, psychobiological phenomenon, the anthropologist Allan Young helpfully reminds us that it is actually a discursive invention that arose in a particular historical context: 'The disorder is not timeless, nor does it possess an intrinsic unity. Rather, it is glued together by the practices, technologies, and narratives with which it is diagnosed, studied, treated, and represented and by the various interests, institutions, and moral arguments that mobilized these efforts and resources' (1995: 5). As we saw in Chapter 1, this 'historical product' (Young 1995: 5) has its origins in a number of late-nineteenth- and twentieth-century psychological and medical discourses dealing with Euro-American experiences of industrialization, gender relations, and, especially, modern warfare. The feminist psychotherapist Laura Brown points out that our definitions of trauma have been constructed from the experiences of dominant groups in the West, that is, 'white, young, able-bodied, educated, middle-class, Christian men' (1995: 101). As a result, we have come to understand trauma as 'that which disrupts these particular human lives, but no other' (L. Brown 1995: 101). The psychic suffering inflicted on the socially disadvantaged—members of variously marginalized groups—has stayed under the radar and failed to attract public recognition.

In part, this is due to a mismatch between hegemonic definitions of trauma and the psychological pain suffered by the oppressed, which these definitions were never meant to account for in the first place. Hence, simply applying these ostensibly neutral definitions more widely, beyond the contexts out of which, and for which, they were originally developed, is not an adequate solution. After all, it risks making the specificity of this suffering invisible and unknowable. Some commentators have gone so far as to argue that the uncritical cross-cultural application of Western psychological concepts, common in clinical settings as well as in humanistic trauma scholarship, constitutes a form of cultural imperialism. Such accusations have been levelled in particular in relation to humanitarian programmes that deliver psychological aid during and after international emergency situations. The psychiatrist Derek Summerfield, for example, writes that '[p]sychiatric universalism risks being imperialistic, reminding us of the colonial era when what was presented to indigenous peoples was that there were different types of knowledge, and theirs was second-rate' (2004: 238). In the assumption underlying such humanitarian interventions, that Western-style trauma programmes are necessary to allow disaster-affected populations around the world to cope with their harrowing experiences, Summerfield hears 'a modern echo of the age of Empire, when

Christian missionaries set sail to cool the savagery of primitive peoples and gather their souls, which would otherwise be "lost"' (1999: 1457). Along the same lines, Ethan Watters critiques what he calls 'the grand project of Americanizing the world's understanding of the human mind' (2010: 1), that is, the imposition of American definitions of and treatments for mental disorders as the international standard. He argues, for example, that the Western trauma counsellors who arrived in Sri Lanka following the 2004 tsunami trampled over local ideas about mental illness and healing in their rush to help the victims, and thereby ended up causing them more distress instead of alleviating their suffering.

Though, as we have seen, many of the early proponents of PTSD were social justice activists involved in movements against the Vietnam War or in favour of women's equality, critics allege that the PTSD construct is insufficiently attuned to and even obscures issues of racism, heterosexism, classism, and other forms of ongoing structural oppression as sources of trauma. One key problem is its exclusive focus on sudden, unexpected, catastrophic events, which has in fact characterized the field of trauma research from the very beginning. It has been argued that the punctual or event-based model of trauma enshrined in the *Diagnostic and Statistical Manual of Mental Disorders* (DSM) ignores the chronic psychic suffering caused by the structural violence of racial, sexual, class, and other injustices. The cumulative impact of the often subtle everyday discriminations and humiliations inflicted on the victims of such forms of oppression can be as profound as that of spectacular and instantaneous acts of violence, yet only the latter are generally recognized as traumatic stressors. Another, related limitation of the event-based model, attributable to its rootedness in Western conceptions of personhood, is its tendency to regard trauma as an individual phenomenon. Narrowly focusing on the level of the individual psyche rather than taking into account the wider social situation is particularly problematic in a transcultural context, as in collectivist societies individualistic approaches may be at odds with the local culture. Moreover, by doing so one leaves unquestioned the supra-individual conditions that enable the traumatic abuse, such as political oppression, social exclusion, and economic deprivation. Trauma survivors are seen as sufferers from an illness that can be cured through psychological counselling and thereby stripped of political agency. Issues of social injustice become depoliticized as the need for taking collective action towards systemic change is implicitly negated.

Alternative conceptualizations that have been proposed to capture the normative, quotidian aspects of trauma in the lives of many disempowered people, which typically have collective causes, include insidious trauma (Root 1992; L. Brown 1995), complex PTSD or disorders of extreme stress not otherwise specified (Herman 1992a), type II traumas (Terr 1991), safe-world violations (Janoff-Bulman 1992), oppression-based trauma (Spanierman and Poteat 2005), and postcolonial syndrome (Duran *et al.* 1998). This recent work was anticipated, though, by Frantz Fanon, the black Martinican-born psychiatrist-turned-Algerian revolutionary who can be regarded as a pioneer of postcolonial trauma theory (Craps 2013: 28–31). While completing his residency in France, Fanon wrote about the negative psychological effects of racism and colonialism on people of colour in his first book, *Black Skin, White Masks* (1952; see Fanon 1967). His famous account of encountering racial fear in a white child, an experience that Fanon found psychologically devastating, provides a good example of insidious trauma due to systematic oppression and discrimination. Fanon can also be credited with recognizing the social nature of such traumas and the need for structural and material change in order for genuine healing to take place. He returned to the same topic in the final chapter of *The Wretched of the Earth* (1961; see Fanon 1963), which is more overtly political than *Black Skin, White Masks. The Wretched of the Earth* was published shortly before Fanon's death and after he had joined the Algerian liberation movement, having worked in a hospital in Algiers during the war of independence. Describing the mental distress that colonial violence produces in both Algerians and their French colonizers through a series of psychiatric case studies of patients under his care, he notes that it is not only the war but also the colonial situation that it aimed to end that causes psychological harm. Even in calm periods, he contends, colonialism by its very nature insidiously inflicts psychological wounds on the colonized. Though he is rarely read as a trauma scholar, Fanon's work is a clear precursor of contemporary critiques of the punctuality and the individualizing, psychologizing, pathologizing, and depoliticizing tendencies of the dominant trauma model.

Besides broadening the focus of trauma studies to encompass traumatic experiences of non-Western and minority groups, and revising and expanding hegemonic definitions of trauma accordingly, scholars working to liberate the field from its persistent Eurocentric, monocultural tendencies have in recent years also begun to draw attention to the interrelations between traumatic metropolitan or First World histories, particularly the Holocaust, and traumatic colonial histories. In so doing, they call into question notions of absolute uniqueness and radical incomparability that have led to Western historical traumas being considered in isolation from, and often at the expense of, other historical tragedies. An insistence on the inherent relationality of trauma can already be found in Caruth's field-defining publications from the mid-1990s. As we have seen, in *Unclaimed Experience* she observes that 'history, like trauma, is never simply one's own, that history is precisely the way we are implicated in each other's traumas' (1996: 24), and in *Trauma: Explorations in Memory* she posits that 'trauma itself may provide the very link between cultures' (1995a: 11). Even so, the founding texts of literary trauma theory, including Caruth's own work, are largely focused on a single historical trauma, the Nazi genocide of the European Jews, and rarely venture beyond the boundaries of Europe and the US.

It has fallen to later trauma theorists and critics to forge the kinds of links among traumatic histories hinted at but not pursued by Caruth, Felman and Laub, Hartman, or LaCapra. Over the last decade, a significant amount of literary scholarship has been devoted to the interrelatedness of memories of the Holocaust and other atrocities, which had in fact already engaged the attention of historians, philosophers, sociologists, and other intellectuals since soon after the Second World War; for example, Aimé Césaire's *Discourse on Colonialism* (1950; see Césaire 2000), Hannah Arendt's *The Origins of Totalitarianism* (1951), Paul Gilroy's *The Black Atlantic* (1993) and *Between Camps* (2000), and the work of historians of comparative genocide such as Mark Mazower, A. Dirk Moses, Jacques Semelin, Dan Stone, and Jürgen Zimmerer. Noteworthy works of literary scholarship on comparative trauma include Bryan Cheyette's *Diasporas of the Mind* (2013), Debarati Sanyal's *Memory and Complicity* (2015), Max Silverman's *Palimpsestic Memory* (2013), and Michael Rothberg's *Multidirectional Memory* (2009), with the last proving particularly influential.

Rothberg's study theorizes the co-implication of Holocaust and colonial trauma by illuminating what he calls the 'multidirectional' dimension of (traumatic) memory. He offers an alternative to the 'competitive memory' model according to which the capacity to remember historical tragedies is limited and any attention to one tragedy inevitably diminishes our capacity to remember another. Against this framework, which understands collective memory as 'a zero-sum struggle over scarce resources', he suggests that we consider memory as multidirectional, that is, 'as subject to ongoing negotiation, cross-referencing, and borrowing; as productive and not privative' (2009: 3). The concept of multidirectional memory 'draw[s] attention to the dynamic transfers that take place between diverse places and times during the act of remembrance' (2009: 11). Besides making a theoretical argument against a logic of competitive memory based on the zero-sum game and a historical argument about the inseparability of memories of the Holocaust and colonial violence, Rothberg also puts forward a political argument in *Multidirectional Memory.* He questions the assumed link between collective memory and group identity, and suggests that the productive, intercultural dynamic of multidirectional memory has the potential to create 'new forms of solidarity and new visions of justice' (2009: 5). However, he also recognizes that multidirectional memory can function 'in the interest of violence or exclusion instead of solidarity' (2009: 12). Rothberg refines his theoretical framework in a later article where he lays out a map of multidirectional memory with four quadrants, with equation and differentiation on the 'axis of comparison' and solidarity and competition on the intersecting 'axis of political affect' (2011: 525). More explicitly than his monograph, this article emphasizes that not all forms of multidirectionality are to be celebrated as inherently beneficial and politically progressive; indeed, memory discourses relying on differentiation and solidarity, which in Rothberg's view offer 'a greater political potential' than those that rely on equation and competition (2011: 526), represent only one quadrant on his map, a useful tool for navigating the murky waters of comparative trauma.

While the comparative approach undoubtedly represents one of the most important and necessary innovations in trauma studies, a caveat has to be made. Somewhat paradoxically, the Holocaust remains central to efforts to decentralize Western historical traumas. All of the aforementioned studies take it as their point of comparison, as does the vast majority of scholarship in this area. As a result, our collective efforts to move beyond the logic of the unique, the incomparable, and the unprecedented, which has tended to keep the focus squarely on a genocide committed in Europe by Europeans against other Europeans, may inadvertently prove counterproductive. After all, there is something profoundly paradoxical about considering one particular history to be uniquely suited to challenging the uniqueness paradigm. There is still a need for more comparative work in trauma studies, but it would be salutary, it seems to us, if a greater variety of histories were brought into contact with one another.

BEYOND THE TRAUMA CANON

Another new direction in cultural trauma research is a tendency to study texts that deviate from the modernist aesthetic of fragmentation and discontinuity, adherence to which has long been seen as a requirement for entry into the canon of valued trauma literature. The notion that traumatic experiences can only be adequately represented through the use of experimental, modernist textual strategies, which can be traced back to Theodor Adorno's pronouncements about poetry after Auschwitz, had become received wisdom in trauma theory by the 2000s (Vickroy 2002; Whitehead 2004). Trauma theorists often justify their focus on anti-narrative, non-linear, fragmented forms by pointing to similarities with the psychic experience of trauma: 'Trauma narratives go beyond presenting trauma as subject matter or character study. They internalize the rhythms, processes, and uncertainties of traumatic experience within their underlying sensibilities and structures' (Vickroy 2002: 3). An experience that exceeds the possibility of narrative knowledge, so the logic goes, will best be represented by a failure of narrative. Hence, what is called for is the disruption of conventional modes of representation, such as can be found in modernist and postmodern writing.

Among the first critics to challenge this prescriptive trauma aesthetic were Jill Bennett and Rosanne Kennedy, who warned that it might lead to the unquestioning adoption of a restrictive trauma canon:

> there is a danger that the field is becoming limited to a selection of texts that represent a relatively narrow range of traumatic events, histories and cultural forms, rather than engaging the global scope of traumatic events and the myriad forms that bear witness to them.
>
> (2003: 10)

They denounce the tendency among teachers of trauma literature to choose the texts they assign on the basis of the extent to which they comply with prevailing theories of trauma, as a result of which a wide variety of traumatic experiences and modes of representation remains unknown and unexplored. Realist and indigenous writing in particular rarely make the cut, as they often depart from the unspeakability paradigm, featuring witnesses who claim narrative and political agency rather than being passive, inarticulate victims (Kennedy and Wilson 2003).

Roger Luckhurst has similarly called for received ideas and assumptions about how literature bears witness to trauma to be revised. In *The Trauma Question* (2008), he deplores trauma theory's sole focus on anti-narrative texts, which reproduce the disruptive impact of trauma by formal means. He notes a curious split over the value of narrative between cultural theory and therapeutic discourse: whereas the former is concerned to sustain irresolution and disjuncture and views narrative with suspicion, as a betrayal of the singularity of the traumatic experience, the latter embraces narrative as a means of healing from trauma. While Luckhurst recognizes and respects the different disciplinary imperatives that cultural artefacts and therapeutic work obey, he rejects poststructuralist trauma theory's exclusive valorization of rupture, difficulty, and impossibility, and the resultant wholesale dismissal of the vast number of stories saturating our culture that do in fact transform trauma into a conventional, accessible narrative. Luckhurst points out that the crisis of representation caused by trauma generates narrative *possibility* just as much as narrative *impossibility.* Beyond the narrow canon of high-brow, avant-garde texts, he reminds us, 'a wide diversity of high, middle and low cultural forms have provided a repertoire of compelling ways to articulate that apparently paradoxical thing, the trauma narrative' (2008: 83). In his book, Luckhurst surveys this broad range of testimonial forms, studying popular trauma memoirs and novels by writers like Stephen King alongside more canonical trauma texts, such as the work of Toni Morrison and W. G. Sebald, while also discussing various examples of trauma cinema and photography drawn from across the aesthetic spectrum.

Following in Luckhurst's footsteps, Anne Rothe has published a study of popular trauma culture that looks at misery memoirs, including fake autobiographical narratives of child abuse and Holocaust survival, as well as daytime TV talk shows, ranging from pop-therapeutic shows such as *Oprah Winfrey* and *Phil Donaghue* to sensational talk shows such as *Ricki Lake* and *Jerry Springer.* Rothe reiterates Luckhurst's point that 'narratives of victimization and survival, trauma and recovery are anything but restricted to scholarship in postmodern trauma theory and the select examples from the literary and filmic canon that constitute its limited empirical corpus' (2011: 4). She goes on to argue that 'it is precisely the question that trauma studies scholarship has left out that ought to be explored, namely how the ubiquitous notion of trauma functions in contemporary culture' (2011: 4). While Rothe finds fault with the various popular culture products she studies for staging depoliticizing spectacles of suffering, she maintains that they are worthy of greater attention as the pre-eminent mass media genres for depicting the pain of others.

Another such genre that has begun to attract the interest of trauma scholars lately is that of video games. The last two decades have seen the release of a number of high-profile video games that engage with trauma, whether by putting the player in the shoes of a traumatized person (as in *Trauma*, 2011, and *Max Payne*, 2001), incorporating the structure and aesthetics of trauma into the game mechanics (*Limbo*, 2011), or placing the player in traumatizing situations and requiring them to make impossible choices (*Spec*

Ops: The Line, 2012). In a series of articles analysing some of these games, Tobi Smethurst (Smethurst 2015; Smethurst and Craps 2015; Smethurst 2017) argues that the specific mechanical and aesthetic qualities of the video game medium have to be taken into account if we are to understand how video games mobilize trauma, which differs from the ways in which more established media such as books and films do so. Video games' inherent interactivity, their unique ability to involve the player in the game world, can foster particular kinds of empathy and identification, making them especially well-suited to exploring issues of guilt and complicity.

As the many alternative representational practices mentioned in the previous paragraphs indicate, trauma theory's focus is no longer primarily on the literary or the aesthetic. Despite the field's origins in, and strong affinity with, literary criticism, it is increasingly delving into studying non-literary, non-verbal, popular, and vernacular forms of expression. Particularly prominent among these are visual art, cinema, and photography. This should not come as a surprise, given that trauma theory derives some of its central concepts, such as intrusive images, flash-backs, unprocessed memories, and unconscious registration, from visual culture. Indeed, the understanding of trauma as a literal imprint of an external event can be seen to align trauma theory with the recording technologies of photography and cinema. The field's interest in visual modes of representation is not exactly a new development either, if we think of Cathy Caruth's analysis of *Hiroshima mon amour* (1959) in *Unclaimed Experience* (1996) or Shoshana Felman's discussion of *Shoah* (1985) in *Testimony* (1992), not to mention the widespread attention commanded by video testimony among trauma scholars in the 1990s, but it has definitely intensified, as well as diversified, since the early days. A considerable amount of scholarship has now been devoted to the role of trauma and witnessing in film (Blake 2008; Elsaesser 2014; J. Hirsch 2004; Lowenstein 2005; Kaplan 2005; Kaplan and Wang 2004; Morag 2013; Rastegar 2015; Walker 2005), photography (Baer 2002; M. Hirsch 1997; Sontag 2003), the visual arts (Bennett 2005; Saltzman and Rosenberg 2006; van Alphen 1997), theatre (Plunka 2018), performance (Edmondson 2018), television (Rothe 2011), video games (Smethurst 2015; Smethurst and Craps 2015; Smethurst 2017), the graphic novel (Romero-Jódar 2017), or several of these media together (Guerin and Hallas 2007; M. Hirsch 2012; Luckhurst 2008; Meek 2009). Whether explicitly or implicitly, all these critics call for trauma theory to face up to and fix its aesthetic elitism problem by expanding its realm of analysis beyond a select group of modernist and postmodern literary texts to encompass a much broader range of cultural mediations of trauma.

An additional reason why the field's attachment to a modernist aesthetic is problematic is the shakiness of the underlying assumption that there is a necessary relation between aesthetic form and ethical effectiveness, regardless of context. After all, narrative devices and representational strategies that may once have been experimental and unconventional inevitably become familiar and recognizable conventions with time and through overuse, ossifying into genre clichés. As Gibbs argues in *Contemporary American Trauma Narratives*, the supposedly challenging disruptions to ordered narrative prescribed by the dominant trauma aesthetic have become hackneyed, and consequently their effect has been blunted. In fact, he attributes the persistence of what he calls the 'trauma genre', conventionally unconventional trauma writing, in part to 'a self-reinforcing circuit of fictional and non-fictional prose narratives that exist[] in tandem with a supporting critical structure' (2014: 2). As Lucy Bond (2011; 2015) has also argued, trauma writers borrow from trauma theory to lend their work credibility, while trauma theorists in turn see their positions validated in the convenient mirror of this theory-based literature. Bond identifies 'a lack of self-reflexivity in many of these [9/11] novels, manifested in an uncritical recycling of paradigms inherited from canonical trauma theory, and a corresponding [critical] refusal to note the imbrication of these ideas with wider ideological discourses' (2015: 14). Gibbs describes this as an echo-chamber effect that further entrenches hegemonic assumptions regarding the representation of trauma and its impact. He calls for greater attention to texts that challenge the accepted formulae, such as realist trauma novels or what he calls 'traumatic metafiction' (2014: 31): texts that either ignore or actively undermine the allegedly unconventional conventions of orthodox trauma writing, and which, as a result, may actually be more successful in conveying the experience of trauma and affecting readers.

PERPETRATOR TRAUMA

As a field, trauma theory took shape in the early 1990s partly in response to a sharp increase in the production, institutional collection, and public visibility of testimonies by Holocaust survivors. The work of Geoffrey Hartman, Shoshana Felman and Dori Laub, and Lawrence Langer played a particularly important role in this regard. While trauma theory has traditionally focused on experiences of innocent victimhood, the last few years have seen a redirection of attention to perpetrators of traumatic events. This development is in keeping with a larger cultural trend: a number of phenomena have propelled the complex and troubling issues surrounding the figure of the perpetrator to the centre of scholarly as well as public interest in recent years. These phenomena include a series of high-profile perpetrator trials (such as those of John Demjanjuk, Radovan Karadzic, Slobodan Milosevic, and Charles Taylor), a spate of often controversial films and novels focusing on those responsible for extreme violence and suffering (e.g. *Downfall*, 2004; *The Specialist*, 1999; *The Act of Killing*, 2012; Jonathan Littell's *The Kindly Ones*, 2006; and Bernhard Schlink's *The Reader*, 1995), and the demands of post-conflict reconciliation in numerous societies (such as South Africa, Rwanda, Argentina, Chile, Guatemala, Northern Ireland, Bosnia, and Australia).

However, the notion that perpetrators can be traumatized by their own actions is still highly controversial, even though trauma theory, for all its victim-centredness, has actually taken this for granted right from its inception, albeit apparently unwittingly. Indeed, rather strikingly, some of Caruth's key examples of trauma turn out to be instances of perpetrator trauma, a fact that she does not readily acknowledge. One of these is the story of Tancred and Clorinda, about which LaCapra writes:

> One might observe that her focus on the survivor-victim (indeed, the apparently ambiguous status of Tancred as perpetrator-victim who is termed in passing a survivor) does not explicitly open itself to the formulation of the specific problem of perpetrator trauma which her example seems to foreground ...
>
> (2001: 182)

Another case in point of how an instance of perpetrator trauma surreptitiously comes to stand in for trauma in general was already discussed in Chapter 3: the trauma of the Hebrew people caused by their own murder of Moses, as posited by Freud in his speculative account of the origin of Judaism in *Moses and Monotheism*.

This peculiar feature of Caruth's work has been little noted; however, one critic who—like LaCapra—does point it out, and who is scandalized by it, is Ruth Leys. Leys finds Caruth's analysis of the story of Tancred and Clorinda deficient in many respects, but what is most problematic about it, in her view, is its implication that perpetrators can be trauma sufferers. Her scathing critique of Caruth's analysis culminates in an expression of shock and horror at this suggestion:

> But her discussion of Tasso's epic has even more chilling implications. For if, according to her analysis, the murderer Tancred can become the victim of the trauma and the voice of Clorinda testimony to *his* wound, then Caruth's logic would turn other perpetrators into victims too—for example, it would turn the executioners of the Jews into victims and the 'cries' of the Jews into testimony to the trauma suffered by the Nazis. ... On Caruth's interpretation, what the parable of Tasso's story tells us is that not only can Tancred be considered the victim of a trauma but that even the Nazis are not exempt from the same dispensation.
>
> (2000: 297)

While Leys baulks at the very idea, the existence of perpetrator trauma to which Caruth's interpretation of the Tancred and Clorinda story does indeed point is calmly recognized by LaCapra:

> not everyone traumatized by events is a victim. There is the possibility of perpetrator trauma which must itself be acknowledged and in some sense worked through if perpetrators are to distance themselves from an earlier implication in deadly ideologies and practices.
>
> (2001: 79)

Crucially, though—and this point helps clear up the conceptual confusion underlying Leys's outraged reaction—LaCapra adds: 'Such trauma does not, however, entail the equation or identification of the perpetrator and the victim' (2001: 79). Indeed, the 'psychic proximity' between victim and perpetrator does not make them 'accomplices in the same indistinct gray zone': 'The difference between them is social, ethical, and political, and even the traumatized perpetrator is not a victim in the pertinent ethical and political sense' (LaCapra 2009: 79). As Rothberg points out, Leys makes a 'category error' by 'elid[ing] the category of "victim" with that of the traumatized subject': 'The categories of victim and perpetrator derive from either a legal or a moral discourse, but the concept of trauma emerges from a diagnostic realm that lies beyond guilt and innocence or good and evil' (2009: 90). Calling someone a trauma survivor or a trauma victim does not in and of itself confer any moral superiority on that person, as both victims and perpetrators can suffer trauma, trauma being a morally neutral psychological category.

That, at least, is the theory. In practice, however, the concept of trauma continues to function as a moral judgement in Western society, as it had done for about a century before US psychiatry's reinvention of trauma in the 1980s 'removed the moral dimension from clinical practice' (Fassin and Rechtman 2009: 95). In their anthropological study *The Empire of Trauma: An Inquiry into the Condition of Victimhood*, Didier Fassin and Richard Rechtman point out that the DSM-III steering committee classed the perpetrators of atrocities with the victims by including in PTSD 'the conditions presented by all military personnel affected by the [Vietnam] war, regardless of whether they had suffered or caused the traumatic event' (2009: 92–93). However, Fassin and Rechtman further note that moral evaluation has continued to be reintroduced in the ways in which the concept of trauma is actually used:

> The door may have been shut against moral judgment, but it found its way in through the window. Or rather, it never really left the scene at all. In fact trauma enjoys its current status more as a moral than as a psychological category. ... Rather than a clinical reality, trauma today is a moral judgment. ... trauma today is more a feature of the moral landscape serving to identify legitimate victims than it is a diagnostic category which at most reinforces that legitimacy.
>
> (2009: 284)

While, in strictly clinical terms, it makes sense to argue for the recognition of the phenomenon of perpetrator trauma, in the real world such recognition will effectively be interpreted as making a dubious case for exonerating perpetrators by considering them 'legitimate victims', which amounts to a betrayal of the memory of the real victims. We can insist on the distinction between trauma and victimhood for as long as we want, and with good reason, but the fact remains that the two concepts seem to be inextricably linked in the public consciousness. This partly explains the anxiety concerning the applicability of the concept of trauma to perpetrators as well as actual victims. Gibbs remarks on the irony that, 'while PTSD depended as a concept upon the lobbying of perpetrator trauma sufferers, their particular condition has been marginalised in the years since the acceptance of PTSD as the principal trauma paradigm' (2014: 166).

However, even if trauma and victimhood were to be successfully disentangled, the notion of perpetrator trauma would in all likelihood remain contentious because of the mere fact that it humanizes the perpetrator. After all, by taking the existence of perpetrator trauma as a given, one attributes to perpetrators of atrocities 'a vestige of humanity' that is 'manifested through their trauma' (Fassin and Rechtman 2009: 94). As Fassin and Rechtman point out in relation to Vietnam veterans, their psychological suffering 'show[s] that they still share[] in the humanity that their cruelty would seem to have destroyed' (2009: 94). The claim that perpetrators can be traumatized implies that perpetrators are human beings, just like the rest of us. This is a disturbing implication that sits uneasily with the popular and reassuring idea of perpetrators as incomprehensible, monstrous, demonic, inhuman others. To insist that perpetrator trauma be recognized is to resist such caricatures, which allow us to identify with the victims without a second thought and thereby to avoid the painful truth of humanity's potential for evil. Acknowledging that perpetrators 'may also be traumatized by their experience', LaCapra argues that

> the historian should attempt to understand and explain such behavior and experience as far as possible—even recognize the unsettling

> possibility of such behavior and experience in him- or herself—but obviously attempt to counteract the realization of even its reduced analogues.
>
> (2001: 41)

Perpetrators are real figures, just like victims, and if we refuse to examine their experience, 'we construct them as abstract, mythical figures whose actions cannot be accounted for' (McGlothlin 2010: 214). It is imperative, therefore, for us as critics not to avert our eyes from the perpetrator or to retreat into the comforting and lazy belief that he or she is an incomprehensible monster devoid of humanity or psychological interiority.

In this regard, literary and cultural studies have been lagging behind disciplines such as history, psychology, and philosophy, which have tended to show less reluctance to engage with the perpetrator's perspective. Consider, for example, the work of Raul Hilberg, Hannah Arendt, Christopher Browning, Daniel Goldhagen, Stanley Milgram, Philip Zimbardo, Robert Jay Lifton, Harald Welzer, and Gillian Rose. While literary and cultural studies have been slow to catch up, the last few years have seen the publication of a number of essays and books that explore the ways in which the consciousness of the perpetrator is represented. Essays by Richard Crownshaw (2011), Robert Eaglestone (2010; 2011), Erin McGlothlin (2010; 2014; 2016), Susannah Radstone (2001; 2007a; 2007b), and Sue Vice (2013); an essay collection titled *Representing Perpetrators in Holocaust Literature and Film* (2013) edited by Jenni Adams and Vice; Gibbs's *Contemporary American Trauma Narratives* (2014); Raya Morag's *Waltzing with Bashir: Perpetrator Trauma and Cinema* (2013); and Joshua Pederson's *Sin Sick: Moral Injury in Literature* (forthcoming) all come to mind.

As we already suggested, there is also a growing body of cultural production that lends itself to such analysis—Crownshaw speaks of 'a turn toward the figure of the perpetrator in recent historical fiction' (2011: 75). It seems to us, moreover, that writers and artists are increasingly shedding their inhibitions about exploring the subjectivity of the perpetrator. While Martin Amis's 1989 novella *Time's Arrow* and Schlink's 1995 novel *The Reader*, for example, depict the lives of Holocaust perpetrators but 'ultimately defer any direct, sustained access to their consciousness' (McGlothlin 2010: 224), more recent cultural treatments of perpetration have no such qualms about rendering the perpetrator's mind and inviting the reader, viewer, or player to identify with his perspective. We have in mind works such as Littell's novel *The Kindly Ones*, Amis's short story 'The Last Days of Muhammad Atta' (2006), Rachel Seiffert's novel *Afterwards* (2007), Ari Folman's animated documentary film *Waltz with Bashir* (2008), the third-person shooter video game *Spec Ops: The Line*, and Joshua Oppenheimer's documentary film *The Act of Killing*. In fact, many of these works even explicitly show their respective protagonists to be suffering from post-traumatic stress disorder, something that is clearly the case in *Afterwards, Waltz with Bashir, Spec Ops: The Line*, and *The Act of Killing*.

According to some mental health professionals, though, the PTSD diagnosis may not be adequate to capture the specificity of the psychological suffering experienced by perpetrators. In a 2002 book, Rachel MacNair calls the form of PTSD that is associated with killing in combat, and which tends to be particularly severe, 'perpetration-induced traumatic stress' (PITS). An alternative diagnosis that has gained popularity in recent years is that of moral injury. This concept was coined by psychiatrist Jonathan Shay in the mid-1990s. In his book *Achilles in Vietnam* (1995), which relates the psychic pain of Vietnam veterans to Homer's portrait of Achilles in *The Iliad*, Shay describes moral injury as a result of a betrayal of what is right by an authority figure in a high-stakes situation. In recent years, the concept has been revived and expanded by a wave of psychologists including Brett Litz and his colleagues, who define it as follows:

> *Perpetrating, failing to prevent, bearing witness to, or learning about acts that transgress deeply held moral beliefs and expectations.* This may entail participating in or witnessing inhumane or cruel actions, failing to prevent the immoral acts of others, as well as engaging in subtle acts or experiencing reactions that, upon reflection, transgress a moral code. We also consider bearing witness to the aftermath of violence and human carnage to be potentially morally injurious.
>
> (2009: 700)

Crucially, according to Litz and his team, moral injury results not only from the witnessing of an ethical breach by someone else, as in Shay's account, but also from the commission of or failure to stop one. While similar to PTSD in many ways, moral injury has some distinct symptoms, which Pederson sums up as anger/rage, social isolation, poor self-care, and increasingly negative feelings about the moral value of the self and the world. Both Pederson and Gibbs use the concept in their respective analyses of US creative fiction about the wars in Afghanistan and Iraq, which are said to have led to an increase in moral injury among veterans. Indeed, it is probably no coincidence that Litz *et al.*'s expanded definition was formulated against the backdrop of these chaotic conflicts, characterized by fluid rules of engagement and blurred distinctions between civilians and insurgents. In fact, preliminary evidence suggests that moral injury is also prevalent among operators of unmanned aerial vehicles or drones (Press 2018), which are widely seen as the future of warfare. Pederson and Gibbs argue that the presence of moral injury shapes not only the content but also the form of literary texts, manifesting itself through various types of stylistic and structural excess (Pederson, forthcoming) and non-formulaic literary techniques (Gibbs 2014).

Whatever exact diagnosis one settles on, it is important, we believe, for trauma theory to counteract its questionable tendency to overidentify with innocent victimhood by engaging earnestly and critically with portrayals of perpetrators of atrocities. The aim of this shift or broadening of focus is not to blur vital distinctions such as those between victims and perpetrators and between innocence and guilt or to normalize and excuse extreme violence; rather, it is to stem what Crownshaw calls 'the universalisation of the victim's identity' in trauma theory, which 'compounds the otherness of the perpetrator and obfuscates the processes of perpetration' (2011: 77). Gibbs voices the suspicion that 'the strenuous ethical denial of interest in the perpetrator in cultural trauma studies represents an attempt to deny Americans' possible status as perpetrators' (2014: 159). By leaving unchallenged, or even facilitating, the general appropriation of victim status in the US post-9/11, trauma theory effectively helped legitimize the country's aggressive reaction to the al-Qaeda attacks against the US in 2001 (the so-called War on Terror) and erase the actual victims of US foreign policy

(Gibbs 2014; Bond 2015). Conversely, a trauma theory that allows for identification with perpetration as well as with victimhood, and which thus reminds us of 'the *presumptuousness* of an identification with utter innocence', might 'mitigate (in some small measure) the historical repetition of atrocity by avoiding the Manicheanism and simplification that lie at the heart of Fascism itself' (Radstone 2001: 66).

Besides overcoming its reluctance to consider the very possibility of perpetrator suffering, a responsible trauma theory would also go beyond the victim–perpetrator binary by recognizing the specific experiences of various in-between groups with complicated levels of guilt and complicity such as bystanders, beneficiaries, collaborators, forced perpetrators, victims-turned-perpetrators, and people one or more generations removed from those directly involved in violence in one way or another. Rothberg has recently coined the concept of the 'implicated subject' as an umbrella term identifying some of those various intermediate and alternative forms of involvement. The concept, for Rothberg, names 'a large and heterogeneous collection of subjects who enable and benefit from traumatic violence without taking part in it directly' (2014b). He sees the notion of implication, which is cognate with complicity and privilege, as 'providing a new footing for trauma theory' (2014b). The specific figure of the beneficiary is the subject of Bruce Robbins's eponymous study (2017), which shows how the relatively comfortable, secure, and sheltered lives of inhabitants of the developed world depend on the labour and suffering of people far away.

Another useful starting point for those interested in exploring subject positions beyond victim and perpetrator is the Italian writer and Holocaust survivor Primo Levi's essay 'The Grey Zone' (1989), which contends that binary thinking is inadequate in the face of the complexity of life in the Nazi concentration camps. What Levi calls the 'grey zone' is inhabited by victims who compromise and collaborate with their oppressors in various ways and under varying levels of coercion in exchange for material or other benefits not available to their fellow prisoners. These morally ambiguous 'privileged' prisoners do not constitute a monolithic group but come in many different shades of grey. An extreme example of collaboration on which Levi dwells at some length is that of the *Sonderkommandos* or 'special squads', the groups of prisoners entrusted with the running of the gas chambers and crematoria. Other occupants of the grey zone to whom he devotes special attention are the members of the Jewish councils in the ghettos of Nazi-occupied Eastern Europe, who in effect if not in intention assisted the Nazis in peaceably rounding up Jews.

Public taste has traditionally favoured the reassuringly clear-cut categories of heroes or saints versus traitors or villains, as indicated by the success of mainstream Holocaust films such as Steven Spielberg's *Schindler's List* (1993) and Roberto Benigni's *Life Is Beautiful* (1997), which tend to view the history of the camps in straightforward black-and-white terms. However, there appears to be a new readiness among cultural producers and audiences to tell and listen to the stories of both the *Sonderkommandos* and the Jewish councils, as witness recent high-profile novels and films such as Amis's *The Zone of Interest* (2014), Tim Blake Nelson's *The Grey Zone* (2001), László Nemes's *Son of Saul* (2015), and Claude Lanzmann's *The Last of the Unjust* (2013). The last few years have also seen the publication of a remarkable number of African child-soldier narratives, which similarly trouble easy distinctions between victim and perpetrator and often highlight issues of trauma. These include Ishmael Beah's memoir *A Long Way Gone* (2007) and novels such as Ahmadou Kourouma's *Allah Is Not Obliged* (2006), Emmanuel Dongala's *Johnny Mad Dog* (2005), Uzodinma Iweala's *Beasts of No Nation* (2005), Delia Jarrett-Macauley's *Moses, Citizen & Me* (2005), and Chris Abani's *Song for Night* (2007). There is thus no shortage of cultural portrayals of complicated cases of guilt, complicity, and responsibility whose study could further enrich the field of trauma theory as it seeks to move beyond the victim-perpetrator binary and arrive at a more comprehensive and fine-grained understanding of trauma.

THE TRAUMA OF THE FUTURE

In 2006, the *Onion*, a satirical newspaper, published an article titled 'Report: More US Soldiers Suffering from Pre-traumatic Stress Disorder'. The article notes a rise in 'pre-traumatic stress disorder', a 'future-combat-related' psychological condition afflicting not only reluctant new recruits but all categories of military service personnel in growing numbers. It quotes a fictitious Walter Reed Army Hospital psychologist as saying that they are seeing more victims experiencing 'flash-forwards' of roadside bombings and rocket attacks or repeatedly 'preliv[ing]' landmine explosions and mortar shellings wounding or killing innocent civilians, fellow soldiers, or themselves. The article goes on to interview a soldier who is allegedly suffering from 'acute Pre-TSD' in anticipation of being deployed to Iraq: 'nearly three weeks before reporting to Fallujah, [he] suffers from nightmares in which his potential best friend is beheaded'. Another soldier's Pre-TSD is said to be brought on by the 'proto-memories' of being taken hostage and having to shoot and kill another human being. These soldiers are haunted, apparently, not by traumatic memories of past events but by their own projections of events that they expect to experience or witness during their deployment: possible future events that have not yet taken place. The article ends by pointing out that, according to unnamed researchers, it is not just members of the armed forces who are at risk for Pre-TSD but also other sections of the population, including 'parents of children approaching military age, Iraqi citizens, and any person who watches more than three hours of television news per day'.

The *Onion*'s satirical reporting is sometimes mistaken for real news; in this case, though, it would seem that they really were onto something: by ironically turning the notion of PTSD on its head, the *Onion* had inadvertently identified an actually existing phenomenon. Citing the *Onion* piece in a 2015 article in the scholarly journal *Clinical Psychological Science*, titled 'Pretraumatic Stress Reactions in Soldiers Deployed to Afghanistan', Dorthe Berntsen and David Rubin point out that 'concern for future negative events is to be expected' (2015: 663) given PTSD's status as an anxiety disorder. They argue that pre-traumatic stress reactions such as intrusive images of and nightmares about negative future events, avoidance behaviour, and increased arousal to stimuli associated with the events are 'a real aspect of the phenomenology of PTSD' (2015: 663); a central aspect even, which, however, has so far been largely ignored. Presenting data from Danish soldiers who saw active service in Afghanistan, Berntsen and Rubin demonstrate that pre-traumatic stress exists and that it reliably predicts PTSD symptoms during and after deployment: past-related PTSD symptoms are found to be mirrored by similar future-related PTSD symptoms. Their findings suggest that the prevailing understanding of PTSD as a disorder primarily related to the past needs to be revised, as 'intrusive images and dreams of future events and associated avoidance and increased arousal are experienced to the same extent as reexperiencing, avoidance, and increased arousal associated with past events' (2015: 672).

The notion of pre-traumatic stress is also beginning to make inroads in cultural trauma scholarship. In *Tense Future: Modernism, Total War, Encyclopedic Form* (2015a), for example, Paul Saint-Amour calls for a re-orientation of trauma studies from the past to the future, from memory to anticipation. As he points out, the field lacks 'an account of the traumatizing power of anticipation' (2015a: 17). Due to trauma studies' dependence on a 'largely psychoanalytic chronology' (2015a: 13), the notion of a pre-traumatic syndrome is 'practically nonsensical' as the symptoms of trauma and the syndrome they constitute are 'emphatically and exclusively *post*-traumatic' (2015a: 14). While not oblivious to the future altogether, the field tends to construct it as 'a container for the repetition of past traumas' rather than as 'a vector or agent of traumatization' (2015a: 14n17). Saint-Amour traces this tendency back to Freud, who, in his discussion of shell-shock in *Beyond the Pleasure Principle*, argues that anxiety provides a defence against trauma. Deprived of this defence by a sudden influx of unexpected stimulation, shell-shock victims are condemned to compulsively repeat the painful experience in their nightmares. These restage the overwhelming event in a belated attempt by the psyche to prepare itself for it by triggering the anxiety whose omission was the cause of the trauma. Anxiety, for Freud, is 'a shield against traumatization, not a source of it' (Saint-Amour 2015b). Saint-Amour sets this Freudian theory against critic Lewis Mumford's observations in 1938 of the 'collective psychosis' in a city preparing for war: 'the constant anxiety over war produces by itself a collective psychosis comparable to that which active warfare might develop' (qtd in Saint-Amour 2015a: 6). According to Saint-Amour, it is time for trauma studies to take seriously Mumford's suggestion that the dread of a potentially oncoming disaster can traumatize as much as an actually realized one. It would be wise, he suggests, to take on board 'dissident temporalities' (2015a: 23) theorized elsewhere in the humanities and social sciences, including in fields such as nuclear criticism and queer theory, which reject a linear conception of history powered by biological reproduction and embrace counterintuitive notions of time.

Tense Future is primarily concerned with the prospect of total war in the literature from the interwar period. Saint-Amour argues that the years 1918–1939 were characterized by a pervasive sense of anxious anticipation and were thus experienced 'in real time as an interwar period' (2015a: 8). In the wake of the First World War, the dread of an even more devastating future conflagration saturated the imagination, as evidenced by the cultural production of those years: canonical works of modernist fiction such as James Joyce's *Ulysses* (1922) and Ford Madox Ford's *Parade's End* (1924) are reinterpreted as meditations on impending disaster. In Saint-Amour's reading, they are encyclopedic novels suffused by anticipatory anxiety, which at the same time resist the discourse of total war by offering parodic, incomplete versions of totality. While focusing on the interwar period, Saint-Amour expands the scope of his inquiry to encompass the Cold War and even our own early-twenty-first-century moment; indeed, he characterizes late modernity in its entirety as 'perpetual interwar' (2015a: 305). After all, the experience of simultaneously remembering and expecting war is not unique to the historical interwar period but all too familiar also to those afflicted with anxiety about the prospect of nuclear annihilation or drone strikes.

In a *New York Times* essay that covers some of the same ground as his book, Saint-Amour further specifies that 'war has no monopoly on traumatizing anticipation' (2015b). He points out that other 'storms in our future', such as climate change, can also inflict psychic wounds. The hypothesis that the dread of climate change amounts to a pre-traumatic stress syndrome, a position that is supported by psychiatrist and climate activist Lise Van Susteren (Oberhaus 2017; Van Susteren 2017), is central to another major recent work of cultural scholarship, E. Ann Kaplan's *Climate Trauma: Foreseeing the Future in Dystopian Film and Fiction* (2016). If the more familiar PTSD is 'a condition triggered in the present by past events', pre-trauma, according to Kaplan, describes how 'people unconsciously suffer from an immobilizing anticipatory anxiety about the future' (2016: xix). Like Berntsen and Rubin and Saint-Amour before her, she notes that this phenomenon has been little studied so far, despite its increasing prevalence, and ventures that conceptualizing pre-traumatic stress syndrome (PreTSS) offers 'a new lens for an expanded trauma theory' (2016: 4). Taking a shorter historical view than Saint-Amour, Kaplan posits that we may now be entering a new era characterized by pervasive pre-trauma, in which people live in fear of a catastrophic future marked by environmental crisis. In the absence, as yet, of sound empirical evidence, it is unclear whether this collective anticipatory anxiety does indeed amount to trauma in the clinical sense, which is why it seems safer to regard climate-related PreTSS as a hypothesis for the moment. In this post-9/11 era, media of all kinds bombard us with 'catastrophic futurist scenarios' (Kaplan 2016: xix), inviting audiences to project themselves forward into a post-apocalyptic future world. According to Kaplan, this results in 'a pretraumatized population, living with a sense of an uncertain future and an unreliable natural environment' (2016: xix). She expresses the hope that, rather than paralysing audiences, these dystopian scenarios will serve as a warning and wake-up call to help prevent the apocalyptic outcomes depicted. There is thus an explicit ethical dimension to Kaplan's project of analysing dystopian fictions. Just as in art about past catastrophes such as the Holocaust we witness what must never happen again, she argues in an earlier article, in pre-trauma fictions we witness what must be stopped from happening in the first place (2013: 59).

Kaplan examines a wide range of futurist disaster narratives, both cinematic and literary, that are allegedly capable of inducing pre-traumatic stress. Her prime example, though, is *Take Shelter*, a feature film written and directed by Jeff Nichols and released in 2011 that 'embodie[s] exactly' the phenomenon she is theorizing (2016: 2). Set in small-town Ohio, the film tells the story of a family man and construction worker who is plagued by a series of nightmares and visions foretelling an apocalyptic environmental future. The protagonist's work and family life are thrown into turmoil and his sanity is called into question as a result of these unsettling portents of catastrophic climate change. Steeped in an inexorable air of dread and foreboding, *Take Shelter* perfectly captures for Kaplan 'the psychic state of a human being who is traumatized by imagining future climate catastrophe' (2016: 53–54).

The film's main character is hardly alone, of course, in suffering from anticipatory anxiety about environmental devastation. The media regularly feature stories these days about how gloom is setting in among climate scientists and activists, whose Cassandra-like warnings of impending doom go largely unheeded. Think, for example, of glaciologist Jason Box, who was profiled in *Esquire* after tweeting his alarm at learning that methane plumes were escaping from the sea-floor in the Arctic ocean ('we're f'd'; Richardson 2015); of biologist Camille Parmesan, who announced that she had become 'professionally depressed' as a result of her research on climate change (Thomas 2014); or of civil rights lawyer David Buckel, who died after setting himself on fire at Prospect Park in Brooklyn, New York, to call attention to climate change (Mays 2018). To provide yet another example, in January 2017 the meteorologist and journalist Eric Holthaus got a huge response to a series of fifteen tweets in which he had vented his feelings of despair about our dire environmental predicament and confessed to seeing a counsellor to help him cope with them. Each tweet was retweeted and liked thousands of times, and Holthaus received hundreds of messages from people who told him that they felt the same way (Oberhaus 2017).

Articles and reports about the psychological effects of climate change on the wider population are also increasingly seeing the light of day as the rise in extreme weather events around the world is making the severity of the climate crisis more and more clear. A 2012 report from the National Wildlife Federation concluded that '[a]n estimated 200 million Americans will be exposed to serious psychological distress from climate related events and incidents' (Coyle and Van Susteren 2012: 5). In a recent article in *Nature Climate Change* that resonated with many readers, Ashlee Cunsolo and Neville Ellis coin the term 'ecological grief' to describe 'the grief felt in relation to experienced or anticipated ecological losses, including the loss of species, ecosystems and meaningful landscapes due to acute or chronic environmental change' (2018: 275). Ecological grief, which includes the anticipatory syndrome theorized by the aforementioned scholars, is 'an underdeveloped area of inquiry', according to Cunsolo and Ellis, despite its being

> a natural response to ecological losses ... and one that has the potential to be felt more strongly and by a growing number of people as we move deeper into the Anthropocene [the new geological epoch defined by human impact].
>
> (2018: 275)

As the reality of accelerating climate change becomes inescapable, it is to be expected that pre-traumatic stress and ecological grief more generally will become increasingly common.

We believe that, like the areas we discussed in the previous three sections, pre-trauma represents a site of particularly exciting new research in cultural trauma theory. It goes without saying, though, that the future of humanistic trauma scholarship as we have envisaged it in this chapter is not the future of trauma theory as everyone else sees it or should see it. The new directions on which we have chosen to focus represent a subjective selection from a broader range of possible futures for the field. Moreover, as we will argue in the conclusion, the field would be well advised to proceed with caution and to acknowledge limitations to its explanatory power and utility.

CONCLUSION: THE LIMITS OF TRAUMA

As discussed in Chapter 4, trauma theory is travelling into various kinds of new territory (non-Western or minority trauma, popular culture, the perpetrator experience, and pre-traumatic stress), and these developments, it seems to us, are largely to be applauded. However, trauma theory also needs to guard against overambition and overconfidence in its own explanatory power. While we believe it is vital for trauma theory to go beyond well-trodden paths to previously under- or unexplored terrains, we also have some concerns about unbridled expansion. To save the field from hubristic overreach, it is necessary, we think, to recognize limits to its usefulness and legitimacy.

Our position differs from those of Ruth Leys, Wulf Kansteiner and Harald Weilnböck, and Anne Rothe, who have each launched an all-out attack on trauma theory. Leys's scathing critique of Cathy Caruth's reading of Sigmund Freud and her demolition of what she takes to be the neuroscientific underpinnings of Caruth's brand of trauma theory attempt to completely delegitimize the field that Caruth's work was instrumental in inaugurating. Leys admits her 'impatience with the sloppiness of her [Caruth's] theoretical arguments': 'in the name of close readings she produces interpretations that are so arbitrary, willful, and tendentious as to forfeit all claim to believability' (2000: 305). Moreover, Leys is

> unsympathetic to the way in which she [Caruth] tends to dilute and generalize the notion of trauma: in her account the experience (or non-experience) of trauma is characterized as something that can be shared by victims and nonvictims alike, and the unbearable sufferings of the survivor as a pathos that can and must be appropriated by others.
>
> (2000: 205)

Leys is equally unsparing in her criticism of the work of the neuropsychiatrist Bessel van der Kolk, a leading theorist of PTSD, whom Caruth cites in support of her own claims about trauma. Leys is 'dismayed by the low quality of van der Kolk's scientific work', finding numerous 'slippages and inconsistencies in his arguments about the literal nature of traumatic memory, arguments that are inadequately supported by the empirical evidence he adduces' (2000: 305). Van der Kolk's and Caruth's view of trauma as a literal imprint of an event on the psyche, which is dissociated from normal mental processes of cognition and hence cannot be known or represented, flies in the face of scientific fact, according to Leys, and therefore cannot provide a credible basis for cultural trauma research. The reader of Leys's *Trauma: A Genealogy* (2000) can be forgiven for coming away from the book with the impression that trauma theory as inaugurated by Caruth is an altogether derisory and intellectually hollow if not fraudulent undertaking.

The assault on trauma theory begun by Leys was continued by Kansteiner and Weilnböck in their provocatively titled essay 'Against the Concept of Cultural Trauma Theory (or How I Learned to Love the Suffering of Others without the Help of Psychotherapy)' (2008). They denounce the supposedly ruthless and even cynical aestheticization and valorization of trauma and the callous dismissal of healing and recovery that they claim to find in the work of Caruth and various other trauma theorists. Kansteiner and Weilnböck diagnose what they see as 'a spectacular failure' by humanists and social scientists to develop 'a truly interdisciplinary trauma concept' (2008: 229), for which, in their view, an uncritical attachment to postmodern or poststructuralist theory is to blame. They accuse 'the postmodern trauma discourse' that holds sway in the humanities of 'lack[ing] self-reflexivity' and unquestioningly turning the concept of cultural trauma into 'a new master narrative' (2008: 229). Kansteiner and Weilnböck direct their polemical arrows against a whole range of exponents of this maligned trauma paradigm from around the Western world, while singling out Caruth's influential work for particular criticism. Rejecting what they see as an exuberant celebration of the experience of trauma as providing privileged insight into the human condition, they take Caruth and her followers to task for assuming 'a radical anti-analytical and anti-empirical posture' (2008: 232) and for blithely ignoring the clinical literature on trauma and its treatment. According to Kansteiner and Weilnböck, the belief that 'the trauma experience will and should remain inaccessible to representation' (2008: 231) may be in tune with deconstructive thinking but is not borne out by clinical investigation:

> the indiscriminate rejection of narrative renders the deconstructive trauma paradigm incompatible with the results of clinical research which has shown consistently that integrating traumatic experiences within narrative frameworks is an indispensable tool of psychotherapy and that narrative forms of representation help groups and collective entities to come to terms with events of violence and its mental and social consequences.
>
> (2008: 233)

Kansteiner and Weilnböck go so far as to suggest that Caruth and like-minded scholars are uninterested in if not indifferent to healing and recovery: they allegedly adopt a bystander position that allows them to mentally distance themselves from the psychic suffering of others through idle philosophical speculation detached from reality.

While Kansteiner and Weilnböck clearly do not shy away from hyperbole, Rothe is even more damning in her condemnation of trauma theory. She ramps up the volume in an incendiary essay whose title, 'Irresponsible Nonsense: An Epistemological and Ethical Critique of Postmodern Trauma Theory' (2016), leaves little doubt about the author's position. Aligning herself with Leys as well as Kansteiner and Weilnböck, and expanding on their work, she presents her intervention as 'an external critique' (2016: 181) of the field, delivered by a scholar who does not partake in the discourse she analyses. Rothe thus sets herself apart from scholars such as Karyn Ball, Stef Craps, Geoffrey Hartman, Dominick LaCapra, and Susannah Radstone, who have offered what she characterizes as 'internal critiques'; unlike them, she does not seek to revise and develop trauma theory from within but rejects it outright. As her none-too-subtle title suggests, Rothe also takes her cue from *Fashionable Nonsense: Postmodern Intellectuals' Abuse of Science*, the physicists Alan Sokal and Jean Bricmont's 1997 broadside against the misuse of scientific concepts by postmodern theorists, whom the book aimed to expose as intellectual frauds (Sokal is best known for the hoax he perpetrated against the postmodern journal *Social Text*). The same intent lies behind Rothe's essay, which sets out to unmask trauma theory as just another instance of the kind of pseudo-scientific quackery targeted by Sokal and Bricmont. Tarring its proponents with the same brush wielded by these veterans of the science wars against Jean Baudrillard, Gilles Deleuze, Jacques Lacan, Julia Kristeva, and others, she argues that 'a similarly nonsensical appropriation of scientific research was generated in postmodern trauma theory' and that the 'fashionable transformation of the trauma concept from signifying the psychological aftereffects of extreme violence into a metaphor for a stipulated postmodern crisis of signification is not only epistemologically untenable but also ethically irresponsible' (2016: 182).

Rothe accuses Caruth of using 'misleading interpretations of ideas from disciplines like psychoanalysis, deconstruction, trauma therapy, and the cognitive sciences' to 'authorize her claims' (2016: 182). Following her fellow detractors, Rothe contends that the core theses of trauma theory concerning the inherent unknowability and unrepresentability of trauma are empirically unfounded and at odds with therapeutic discourse, which emphasizes the need for traumatic memories to be narratively integrated if they are to lose their hold over the sufferer. This approach to trauma is unethical, according to Rothe, in that it lessens the representational authority of victims: trauma theorists 'dispossess victims and survivors of the subject position of witness in order to ascribe it to themselves and the status of testimony to their self-aggrandizing speculations' (2016: 192–93);

moreover, they 'efface[] the categorical distinction between perpetrator and victim by ascribing trauma status to the perpetrator's experience and casting victims in the perpetrator position because they can supposedly only convey their own trauma by traumatizing others' (2016: 192).

If anything, the intensity, vehemence, and persistence of these critiques are a testament to trauma theory's considerable importance as a field of academic study: only a paradigm perceived to be dominant is likely to attract this level of hostility. While we are sympathetic to some of Leys's, Kansteiner and Weilnböck's, and Rothe's micro-arguments, we do find much of value in trauma theory and so do not see any need to reject the entire enterprise. Even though we have some reservations ourselves, we have no desire to be associated with the backlash against trauma theory; we do not want to throw the baby out with the bath water. Our position, in other words, is one of appreciative but critical engagement, or internal rather than external critique, to employ Rothe's useful distinction. The main problem that we see, and that we believe the field needs to do more to confront, is that the prevalence of the concern with trauma threatens to displace positive memories and oversimplify complex global problems with potentially depoliticizing results. The field keeps expanding and reinventing itself, and has to do so if it is to stay relevant in the globalized world of the twenty-first century, but at the same time it needs to be more self-reflexive about the limits of this endeavour.

For one thing, while trauma theory is quick to interpret people's responses to extreme events in terms of post-traumatic stress disorder, it is important to realize that other kinds of responses are possible. As Roger Luckhurst points out, 'PTSD has a shadow condition that has been theorized in parallel with the emergence of trauma: resilience', which is defined as '*positive adaptation within the context of significant adversity*' (2008: 210). He questions the tendency to pathologize signs of resilience as evidence of 'absent grief' (2008: 210) and to assume that 'the impossible, aporetic or melancholic response is the only appropriately ethical condition for individuals and communities defined by their post-traumatic afterwardsness' (2008: 211–12). An alternative to PTSD that is closely related to resilience and that has also gained traction in recent years is the concept of post-traumatic growth, which was coined by the psychologists Lawrence Calhoun and Richard Tedeschi in the 1990s to describe 'positive change that the individual experiences as a result of the struggle with a traumatic event' (1999: 11). Post-traumatic growth tends to be associated with changes in the domains of self-perception, interpersonal relationships, and life philosophy. It can take the form of greater appreciation for life, closer relationships with others, seeing new opportunities in life, a sense of increased personal strength, and positive spiritual change.

While the increased attention to resilience and post-traumatic growth serves as a welcome reminder of the plurality of responses to trauma, which has tended to be overlooked, these categories are best approached with a sceptical eye insofar as they (are used to) promote political quietism. As Luckhurst points out, resilience 'is not really the basis … for any form of cultural or political critique' (2008: 211). Indeed, we suspect that the current popularity of these concepts has much to do with their compatibility, at least in some accounts, with classic bootstrap logic, placing the burden of success or failure on the individual's character and letting the traumatizing system off the hook. That being said, the notion of post-traumatic growth is not destined to be depoliticizing and unthreatening to the established order; indeed, attempts are currently being made to overcome some of its limitations by extending the theory to the collective level, making it more culturally sensitive, and foregrounding long-term, structural as well as punctual forms of trauma (Grayson 2017; Grayson 2018; Williamson Sinalo 2018).

Proponents of resilience and post-traumatic growth can be seen to counter the overemphasis on PTSD by foregrounding other possible memorial relations to the past that have tended to be ignored, dismissed, or misinterpreted. A related concern, which has frequently been voiced in recent years by scholars active in the broader field of memory studies, is that the tendency to confine our understanding of memory to trauma comes at the expense of 'happy' memories. 'Increasingly', Michael Lambek and Paul Antze noted back in 1996, 'memory worth talking about—worth remembering—is memory of trauma' (1996: xii). As Carrie Hamilton observes, this privileging of trauma leads to 'the marginalization of activist memories' (2010: 266). Trauma displaces positive legacies of past activisms, memories of mass movements for change such as the student protests of 1968 or the revolutions of 1989. The close association of memory with trauma can be seen as symptomatic, in Kristin Ross's words, of a general 'reluctance to consider the very notion of politics or collective political agency in the present' (qtd in Hamilton 2010: 269). Hamilton therefore argues for 'caution in the face of the popularity of trauma' (2010: 275). Rather than suggesting that the concept be abandoned altogether, she calls for trauma and related concepts to be 'deployed in ways that make their own histories and politics more transparent' and asks that 'trauma not be allowed to displace other theories and models of memory' (2010: 276). Instead of mourning for what is lost, she writes, memory scholars committed to progressive politics would do well to explore the richness of activist memories, which have been relatively ignored.

This call for a re-orientation of memory studies away from trauma and towards positive memories is echoed by Anna Reading and Tamar Katriel. Noting the historical relationship between the rise of the field and the atrocities of the twentieth century, they are appreciative of the change of focus from commemorations of the heroics of war to the acknowledgement of victim suffering in memory studies. However, in their view, too, this focus on violence, trauma, and victimhood has become limiting and now needs to be challenged, as it has led to 'the obfuscation of the close links that exist between memory-work and political agendas for social change' (2015: 3). They foreground an alternative domain of memory work that has rarely been addressed: memories of non-violent resistance, which can inform and inspire future struggles for social justice. Framing their intervention as offering 'a critique of the body of work within memory studies that has its origins in "trauma studies" and that examines the traumatic impact of violent events and their articulation through various forms of cultural memory' (2015: 9), they see their work as marking a new departure for the field by moving beyond trauma:

> we suggest the importance to memory studies of understanding memory not in terms of trauma, and the repression and working through of violent pasts, but in terms of the value of remembering human agency and the resilience with which individuals and societies

> continue to articulate memories of nonviolent struggles for human dignity, human equality, human freedom.
>
> (2015: 10)

Building on this emerging interest in the nexus of memory and activism, Ann Rigney similarly promotes a 'positive turn' (2018: 370) in memory studies, which she also views as being hampered by an overemphasis on trauma, victimization, and grievance. The field, she writes, has been dominated by 'a traumatic paradigm that both responds to, and feeds into, the predominance of mourning and memorialisation in contemporary cultures of memory' (2018: 369). Following Andreas Huyssen and Enzo Traverso, Rigney ascribes this 'collective state of depression' (2018: 369) to an inability to imagine the future resulting from the failure of the grand narratives that sustained utopian thinking in the last century. The utopian dreams of the first half of the twentieth century have turned sour: our trust in progress has been badly shaken by the Holocaust, the Gulag, and, more recently, the economic crisis. While Rigney believes that memory culture and the study of memory will continue to focus on 'the bad stuff' (2018: 369) for the foreseeable future, she thinks it is time 'to think critically about the cost of this apparently natural link between memory and trauma, lest we become definitively locked into it' (2018: 369). She fears that the fixation on violence and its legacies 'forecloses an awareness of alternative modes of remembrance and alternative traditions of recall. More specifically, it leaves memory studies at risk of losing the ability to capture, wherever it does occur, the transmission of positive forms of attachment' (2018: 369–70). The challenge, according to Rigney, is for the field to become more forward-looking by going beyond its present focus on traumatic memories while steering clear of grand narratives.

We accept the point made by Hamilton, Reading and Katriel, and Rigney that trauma's domination of the field of memory studies risks displacing memories of how people manage to overcome adversity and successfully fight injustice. However, it would be wrong to infer from this that an emphasis on trauma cannot but have politically debilitating effects, as seems to be implied by critics such as Mark Seltzer, Wendy Brown, Lauren Berlant, and John Mowitt. According to Seltzer, the pathological public sphere defined by our contemporary 'wound culture' is inhabited by individuals who indulge in a voyeuristic fetishism of the other's wounds. As we saw in Chapter 1, it is marked by 'the public fascination with torn and open bodies and torn and opened persons, a collective gathering around shock, trauma, and the wound' (Seltzer 1998: 1). Witnessing the suffering of others is not conducive to any kind of progressive social or political change, in Seltzer's view—quite the contrary even: the cultural fixation on spectacles of suffering and trauma, such as car crashes or serial killings, is all about individuals indulging in erotic pleasure, enjoying a sadistic identification with violence and a masochistic identification with exposed pain. In Seltzer's account, the popularity of trauma theory is but an enactment of this morally dubious fascination with trauma as spectacle that is pervasive in the culture at large.

Serious misgivings about the political value and efficacy of focusing on trauma and testimony have also been voiced by Berlant and Brown, who deplore 'the steady slide of political into therapeutic discourse' (W. Brown 1995: 75) that, in their view, the application of notions of trauma to situations of social injustice and the resulting tendency to 'overidentif[y] the eradication of pain with the achievement of justice' (Berlant 2002: 108) aid and abet. Expanding on Brown's work, Mowitt regards the institutional success of trauma theory as symptomatic of 'the troubling contemporary tendency to displace the political with the ethical' (2000: 272–73). The link that has been forged between traumatic injury and moral authority has led to what Mowitt calls 'trauma envy', a general phenomenon of which the rise of the academic study of trauma is just one manifestation. The moral high ground presupposed by trauma theory authorizes a mode of criticism that calls for moral redress but in so doing steers us away, according to Mowitt, from the essential political task of fundamentally questioning, challenging, and transforming the conditions responsible for the trauma.

Cogent though these various critiques are, it seems to us that trauma theory is not destined to serve as the handmaiden of the status quo or as a mere academic alibi for the indulgence of voyeuristic inclinations. On the contrary, we would argue, it can help make visible and intelligible the suffering of individuals and communities, assist us in identifying and understanding situations of exploitation and abuse, bring them to a wider public consciousness, and act as an incentive for the kind of sustained and systemic critique of societal conditions called for by Berlant, Brown, and Mowitt. While a culture of sentimentality is indeed suspect insofar as feeling is made to function as a substitute for political action, empathy with the pain of others can also serve as a motivation for working towards genuine change. The direct-action AIDS movement ACT UP, the Black Lives Matter movement against police brutality in the United States, and the #MeToo movement against sexual harassment and assault, all of which wed mourning to militancy, would seem to be cases in point of how trauma and meaningful activism are not necessarily in contradistinction to each other.

Having said that, we also think it is important for trauma theory not to overestimate its ability to diagnose, let alone solve, the problems that plague the world today, such as exploitation in an age of globalized neoliberal capitalism and the devastations caused by human-induced climate change. These two examples are discussed by Michael Rothberg in his insightful preface to *The Future of Trauma Theory* (2014a). As Rothberg points out, both problems involve punctual as well as 'slow' forms of violence: think of deadly factory fires or collapses in Bangladesh and of extreme environmental events such as Hurricane Sandy on the one hand, and of the everyday exploitation and inhumane working conditions of factory workers in the global South and of gradual environmental degradation on the other. While both forms of violence can have a traumatic impact, it is questionable whether trauma theory provides the only, or best, lens for exploring such complex global problems, which demand 'multi-faceted, interdisciplinary approaches' (2014a: xvi). As Rothberg writes,

> not all violence and suffering are best described by trauma—even if something we can recognize as trauma often accompanies those other forms of violence and suffering. Exploitation and ecological devastation can be traumatic—and can certainly lead indirectly to trauma of various sorts—but their essence (also) lies elsewhere. We need better ways of understanding how different forms of suffering and violence may inhabit the same social spaces and we need to

> understand what such overlap entails for the possibilities of resistance, healing, and social change.
>
> (2014a: xvii)

Rothberg proposes thinking of the trauma category as '*necessary-but-not-sufficient*' (2014a: xvii) for understanding and addressing these kinds of global challenges. Moreover, if trauma theory is to get any kind of critical purchase on them, it will have to reflect, he adds, on '*implicated subject positions* beyond those of perpetrator and victim, such as the beneficiaries of neoliberal capitalism and the inhabitants of the Anthropocene' (2014a: xvii). What he means by this is that trauma scholars are not outsiders to these issues of economic exploitation and environmental destruction but are implicated in them, as consumers of cheap clothes and gadgets made in the global South or as members of a species of planet Earth who both affect and are affected by climate change. If trauma theory is to be of any help at all in addressing these knotty problems, it will have to move beyond the victim-perpetrator binary and take into account various intermediate and alternative forms of involvement, as discussed in Chapter 4.

In conclusion, while we do believe that there is a future for trauma theory, especially if it continues along the road of pluralization and diversification, we think care should be taken to avoid making grandiose claims for the relevance and utility of even a maximally pluralized and diversified trauma theory. Put simply, our argument is that travel is good in many ways—it is important for trauma theory to leave its comfort zone and venture into pastures new—but that there is such a thing as travelling too far. Trauma may be a catchword of our time, but its study does not therefore hold the key to understanding reality and fixing the world's problems. We argue in favour of responsible expansion and against imperial hubris. Trauma theory would do well to show some humility and to accept that it is but one possible mode of inquiry among others, valuable but only in consort with other approaches and methodologies, which it cannot and must not displace.

GLOSSARY

Acting-out Being haunted or possessed by the past, and compulsively reliving the traumatic events of the past in the present, for example in flashbacks or nightmares. The distinction between past, present, and future collapses; one exists in the present as if one were still fully in the past, without any prospect or hope about the future. Cultural trauma researchers usually attribute the term to Dominick LaCapra, who borrows it—along with its counterpart **working-through**—from Sigmund Freud and applies it to the realm of culture.

Collective trauma A group response to a violent or overwhelming occurrence. Theorists of collective trauma, such as Sigmund Freud and Cathy Caruth, generally suggest that the social disruption that follows a traumatic event closely resembles the psychological upheaval experienced by traumatized individuals.

Complex post-traumatic stress disorder (C-PTSD) Similar to but distinct from **post-traumatic stress disorder (PTSD)**, C-PTSD is an anxiety disorder that can develop in response to prolonged and repeated trauma such as chronic sexual abuse or domestic violence. First described by the feminist psychiatrist Judith Herman in the early 1990s, it is alternatively referred to under the rubric of disorders of extreme stress not otherwise specified (DESNOS).

Cultural trauma Ron Eyerman and Jeffrey Alexander use the idea of cultural trauma to refer to the representational processes through which a particular memory or event is labelled as traumatic by a given social group (in the sense that it is regarded as threatening the existence of the collective or as violating one of its central values). While theories of **collective trauma** foreground the similarity between individual and group responses to traumatic events, accounts of cultural trauma argue that collective consciousness does not function in the same way as an individual psyche. Cultural traumas do not result from a shared psychological reaction; rather, in order to be socially accepted as traumatic, an event must be constructed as such by the discourses of the public sphere.

Differend A term coined by Jean-François Lyotard to describe a wrong or injustice that arises because the dominant discourse precludes the possibility of its expression.

Dissociation Taken from Pierre Janet, dissociation describes the separation of normally related mental processes, which leads in extreme cases to disorders such as multiple personality. Most often triggered by a traumatic event, dissociation leads to the production of various symptoms, including hallucinations, sleep walking, and nightmares, through which the subject attempts to rid themselves of an **idée fixe**—an idea or memory by which they have become possessed.

Ecological grief Grief felt in relation to actual or expected ecological losses such as the disappearance, degradation, or death of species, ecosystems, or landscapes. This phenomenon, which has been described by Ashlee Cunsolo and Neville Ellis, is likely to become increasingly common as the world moves ever closer to climate and ecological breakdown.

Historical trauma Dominick LaCapra uses the idea of historical trauma to identify specific instances of suffering and loss (e.g. the Holocaust or 9/11). LaCapra argues that, because it derives from an identifiable event or experience, historical trauma is open to various processes of **working-through** that would allow the traumatized subject to reconnect to the present and the future. By contrast, the related concept of **structural trauma** refers not to a specific event or experience, but to an originary absence that cannot be overcome.

Hysteria In the nineteenth century, hysteria was a catch-all term for a wide range of mental disorders that resulted in symptoms including, but not limited to, nervousness, hallucinations, ungovernable emotional outbursts, various libidinal desires, and **dissociation**. Hysteria was initially associated with affluent women. However, the groundbreaking work of Jean-Martin Charcot identified hysterical symptoms in working-class men injured in railway or industrial accidents. Charcot believed that hysteria occurred when a hereditary predisposition to mental neurosis was activated by a traumatic event. His insistence on the hereditary nature of hysteria was challenged by later psychoanalysts, including Sigmund Freud.

Idée fixe Pierre Janet used the concept of idées fixes to describe ideas or beliefs by which traumatized individuals have become possessed. Janet believed that these mental preoccupations emerged as the result of a traumatic experience. An idée fixe often leads to a process of **dissociation**, through which the subject attempts to split the traumatic memory from everyday consciousness in order to divest it of its psychological power.

Implicated subject A term introduced by Michael Rothberg for various categories of people who enable and benefit from traumatic violence without being directly involved in it as either victim or perpetrator.

Insidious trauma Coined by Maria Root and developed by Laura Brown, the concept of insidious trauma names the psychological effects of experiences of normative, everyday forms of oppression (such as sexism, racism, homophobia, classism, and ableism) that do not meet the traditional diagnostic criteria for **post-traumatic stress disorder (PTSD)**.

Grey zone A metaphorical concept used by Primo Levi to denote the space between 'pure' victims and perpetrators in the Nazi concentration camps and beyond. It is inhabited by victims who compromise and collaborate with their oppressors in one way or another and with varying levels of responsibility in return for material benefits or other privileges.

Latency The period of time that elapses between the occurrence of a traumatizing event and its registration as a psychological experience. In *Studies on Hysteria* (1895), Sigmund Freud and Josef Breuer argued that the mental effects of an event, such as an early sexual encounter, would not be felt until they were triggered by a second occurrence, which might take place many years after the first. Although many of Freud's legacies have proved contentious, most contemporary theories of trauma continue to emphasize the belatedness of traumatic experience.

Melancholia A response to loss characterized by an inability to let go of the lost object and to re-engage with life. The melancholic cannot acknowledge and accept the need to move on. They internalize the lost object in a self-destructive attempt to remain loyal to it. In contrast to **mourning**, melancholia, which is related to **acting-out**, is an endless process that prevents one from finding substitution for one's loss. In accordance with Sigmund Freud's ideas in his essay 'Mourning and Melancholia' (1917), melancholia is traditionally seen as a pathological reaction to loss, while mourning is regarded as the healthy alternative.

Microaggressions Everyday and often unintentional verbal or behavioural slights, insults, and indignities that reveal biases against marginalized groups such as people of colour, women, or LGBTQ individuals and leave their victims feeling uncomfortable or distressed. Microaggressions can be a source of **insidious trauma** for members of marginalized groups who are chronically exposed to them.

Moral injury The psychological distress associated with perpetrating, failing to prevent, or witnessing acts that violate one's moral code, typically in the context of military combat. The concept was coined by Jonathan Shay in the mid-1990s and recently expanded by Brett Litz and others against the backdrop of the chaotic wars in Afghanistan and Iraq, which led to an increase in moral injury among veterans. While similar to **post-traumatic stress disorder (PTSD)**, moral injury has some distinct symptoms of its own.

Mourning A response to loss in which a person deals with the grief of losing a loved one or an ideal by letting go of the lost object and eventually replacing it. Closely related to **working-through**, mourning as theorized by Sigmund Freud in his essay 'Mourning and Melancholia' (1917) is typically considered a normal and healthy process of grieving a loss, unlike its conceptual counterpart **melancholia**.

Multidirectional memory A conception of memory marked by transcultural borrowing, exchange, and adaptation. Developed by Michael Rothberg in an eponymous monograph (2009), multidirectional memory draws attention to 'the dynamic transfers that take place between diverse places and times during the act of remembrance'. Rothberg identifies a mutually enabling relationship between Holocaust memory and memories of the struggle for decolonization. He argues that multidirectional memory has the potential to create 'new forms of solidarity and new visions of justice'.

Oedipus complex A cornerstone of Freud's theory of psychosexual development. Freud suggests that, around the ages of three to five, a child will experience feelings of desire for his or her opposite-sex parent while sustaining jealousy and anger towards their same-sex parent. This term was inspired by Sophocles's ancient Greek tragedy *Oedipus Rex*, in which the protagonist unwittingly murders his father and marries his mother.

Perpetrator trauma The phenomenon of perpetrators being traumatized by their own violent actions. While there has been a shift or broadening of focus in trauma studies from victimhood to perpetration lately, the notion that those responsible for inflicting suffering on others can also be traumatized by their experience remains controversial. Due to the common association of trauma with victimhood, using the words 'perpetrator' and 'trauma' in the same breath is often interpreted as making a dubious case for exonerating the perpetrators and as betraying the memory of the actual victims in the process. Other diagnostic categories besides **post-traumatic stress disorder (PTSD)** that have been proposed to capture the specificity of the psychological suffering experienced by perpetrators include perpetration-induced traumatic stress (PITS) and **moral injury**.

Postmemory Marianne Hirsch originally used the concept of postmemory to describe how the children of trauma survivors inherit traumatic memories of events from their parents. Hirsch argues that certain traumas (especially the Holocaust) hold such power over the second generation that they come to experience indirect or mediated recollections of events they did not live through. These traces of the past are likely to be encountered in textual, photographic, or narrative form. More recently, Hirsch has expanded her definition of postmemory beyond the scope of the family, rendering the revised concept more akin to Alison Landsberg's **prosthetic memory.**

Post-traumatic growth The notion, theorized by Lawrence Calhoun and Richard Tedeschi in the 1990s, that individuals can experience positive effects following traumatic events. These effects can manifest in the domains of self-perception, interpersonal relationships, and life philosophy. While the focus in post-traumatic growth research has tended to be on individuals, raising suspicions about the concept's implication in neoliberalism, attempts are being made to extend the theory to the collective level and to make it more culturally sensitive.

Post-traumatic stress disorder (PTSD) This condition was first recognized in the third edition of the American Psychiatric Association's *Diagnostic and Statistical Manual of Mental Disorders* (DSM-III) in 1980. DSM-III defined PTSD as a psychological reaction to an event that is 'outside the range of normal human experience' and cited a number of symptoms (including recurrent and intrusive recollections, dreams, and a heightened sensitivity to external stimuli) that might follow from this experience. DSM-III was influential in terms of legitimizing trauma as a medical condition. However, it has since been criticized for the restrictive terms in which PTSD is defined.

Pre-traumatic stress The traumatizing impact of future (rather than past) catastrophic events. The idea of a psychic wounding produced by the anticipation of violence has been put forward by Paul Saint-Amour in relation to an interwar period haunted by the prospect of a second world war even more devastating than the first one. E. Ann Kaplan, for her part, sees pre-traumatic stress syndrome (PreTSS)—a back-formation of **post-traumatic stress disorder (PTSD)**—as a defining condition of human beings living in the current era of climate change, with its looming threat of ecological disaster. While there is some clinical support for the existence of such a disorder in relation to combat situations, as yet no sound empirical evidence exists demonstrating that the dread of climate change amounts to a pre-traumatic stress syndrome, which is why it is safer to speak of a hypothesis for now.

Prosthetic memory Alison Landsberg's theory of prosthetic memory argues that the technologies of mass culture (films, novels, museums, etc.) have made it possible for individuals and groups to acquire memories of events of which they have no direct lived experience.

Psychodynamic Psychodynamic approaches to psychology explore the unconscious forces that shape human behaviour, giving particular attention to the ways that childhood experiences inform personality development. Such practices are often grounded in Freudian psychoanalytic theory.

Railway spine A medical condition first identified by John Erichsen in 1866. Erichsen argued that the spinal damage that was sustained by victims of railway accidents had both physical and psychological consequences. His thesis was taken up by other medical experts, including Herbert Page, who suggested, even more radically, that the psychological effects of railway accidents were capable of inducing lasting neurosis, whether or not the patient had sustained any physical injuries. In linking physical and psychological injury, theories of railway spine were an important precursor to Jean-Martin Charcot's work on **hysteria** and Hermann Oppenheim's work on **traumatic neurosis**.

Repetition compulsion Sigmund Freud defined repetition compulsion as 'the desire to return to the earlier state of things'. In vernacular parlance, it is most commonly understood as an irresistible tendency to repeat an emotion or event by re-enacting the initial experience or putting oneself in situations where it is likely to reoccur. In relation to trauma, repetition compulsion denotes the way that traumatic memories may return, unbidden, to consciousness in displaced forms such as dreams, flashbacks, or hallucinations.

Resilience Positive adaptation to distressing life circumstances. Closely related to **post-traumatic growth**, resilience is the ability to cope with negative emotions arising from adversity and to continue to function as normal.

Secondary or vicarious traumatization Secondary or vicarious traumatization may occur when an individual or group experiences traumatic symptoms after having been exposed to a representation of an event that they have not themselves lived through. Trigger factors may include media footage (as in the case of 9/11), survivor testimony, or other forms of cultural representation, including novels, films, museums, etc.

Secondary or vicarious witnessing Similar to **secondary or vicarious traumatization**, secondary or vicarious witnessing describes an encounter with the memories of another person or group. Both **postmemory** and **prosthetic memory** are types of secondary witnessing. Most often, these processes take place in mediated form, through engagement with cultural artefacts such as testimony, literature, film, and museums. Recent critiques have raised concern about the ethics of vicarious witnessing, suggesting that such practices can become appropriative or exploitative if they are not engaged in reflexively.

Shell-shock First coined as a term in 1917, shell-shock is the most common label used to refer to the trauma suffered by soldiers in the First World War. It was initially thought to result from physical nerve damage, but the persistence of severe symptoms in individuals who had not seen live combat made it evident that many patients' injuries were predominantly psychological in nature. Shell-shock was never recognized as an official condition, and the treatment of soldiers varied enormously depending on their institutional and national contexts.

Structural trauma Dominick LaCapra uses the concept of structural trauma to denote the psychological impact of foundational absences. Such absences, which might be ontological, ideological, theological, or referential in nature, are transhistorical and unbridgeable. Unlike the legacies of discrete historical losses, structural traumas are not respondent to processes of **working-through** that aim to alleviate the effects of **historical trauma**.

Transference A psychological phenomenon during which an individual unconsciously redirects emotions from one person to another. Transference frequently occurs in a therapeutic environment when the patient receiving treatment projects feelings towards a third person onto their therapist. Often, these encounters involve relationships from the patient's childhood. In cases involving trauma, transferential processes can also inform processes of **secondary or vicarious witnessing**, as the witness (who may or may not be a mental health professional) appears to assimilate the memories and emotions of the traumatized subject.

Trauma envy Envy of the moral authority supposedly bestowed by trauma on anyone who can lay claim to a significant wound, which is seen to give them the power to silence the political demands or resentments of others. According to John Mowitt, who coined the term, such authority is 'the gain of pain'.

Traumatic neurosis First introduced in Hermann Oppenheim's study of railway and industrial accidents, traumatic neurosis is used to describe the lasting pathological symptoms that derive from an intense emotional shock, which often manifest as a kind of **repetition compulsion**. While Oppenheim's work proved unpopular among his contemporaries, the idea of traumatic neurosis was later taken up by Sigmund Freud, who combined it with a libidinal theory of trauma. More recently, traumatic neurosis has been understood as a conceptual precursor to **post-traumatic stress disorder (PTSD)**.

Trigger warning A message presented to an audience, often in an educational context, to warn it that a literary text or other work of art contains potentially distressing content, which may trigger an anxiety response in those who have **post-traumatic stress disorder (PTSD)**. While trigger warnings are becoming increasingly common in contemporary culture, they have caused controversy in academic circles and beyond. Some argue that they are empowering in that they allow vulnerable individuals to psychologically prepare for or avoid disturbing material. Others consider trigger warnings harmful, as they allegedly undermine **resilience**, increase vulnerability, and limit academic freedom.

War neurosis The term that Hermann Oppenheim used to characterize the psychological experience of soldiers during the First World War. Oppenheim suggested that war neurosis was an example of the broader category of **traumatic neurosis**, on which he had worked in the late nineteenth century. War neurosis is another term for **shell-shock** and was used throughout the Second World War in military psychiatry. It was one of a series of concepts that were recategorized under the banner of **post-traumatic stress disorder (PTSD)** in 1980.

Working-through A process of coming to terms with trauma and moving beyond it. It enables one to distinguish between past and present, to relegate traumatic memories to the past, and to realize that one is living here and now with openings to the future. Working-through is seen as a salutary alternative to its conceptual counterpart **acting-out**, which traps one in the past. However, the two processes do not simply stand in opposition to one another. As Dominick LaCapra, who borrows both terms from Sigmund Freud, points out, working-through requires and presupposes acting-out: some degree of acting-out is unavoidable and even necessary.

Wound culture A description of contemporary society introduced by Mark Seltzer in the late 1990s that sees it as addicted to spectacles of violence and public displays of trauma. Fascinated by physical and psychological trauma, the individuals inhabiting this 'pathological public sphere' require repeated exposure to images of wounding, which are endlessly reproduced in films, magazines, talk shows, etc.

Bibliography

Adams, Jenni and Sue Vice, eds (2013) *Representing Perpetrators in Holocaust Literature and Film*, London: Vallentine Mitchell.

Adorno, Theodor (1980) 'Commitment', in Ronald Taylor (ed.), *Aesthetics and Politics*, trans. Francis McDonagh, London: Verso, pp. 177–95.

Adorno, Theodor (1981) 'Cultural Criticism and Society', in *Prisms*, trans. Samuel Weber and Shierry Weber, Cambridge, MA: MIT Press, pp. 17–34.

Alexander, Jeffrey C. (2004) 'Toward a Theory of Cultural Trauma', in Jeffrey Alexander *et al.*, *Cultural Trauma and Collective Identity*, Berkeley, CA: University of California Press, pp. 1–30.

Alexander, Jeffrey C. (2012) *Trauma: A Social Theory*, Cambridge: Polity.

American Psychiatric Association (1980) *Diagnostic and Statistical Manual of Mental Disorders*, third edn (DSM-III), Washington, DC: American Psychiatric Association.

American Psychiatric Association (1987) *Diagnostic and Statistical Manual of Mental Disorders*, third edn, revised (DSM-III-R), Washington, DC: American Psychiatric Association.

American Psychological Association (2001) 'Coping with Terrorism', http://www.apa.org/helpcenter/terrorism.aspx.

Arendt, Hannah (1951) *The Origins of Totalitarianism*, New York: Harcourt Brace Jovanovich.

Baer, Ulrich (2002) *Spectral Evidence: The Photography of Trauma*, Cambridge, MA: MIT Press.

Barker, Pat (2013) *The Regeneration Trilogy*, London: Penguin.

Balaev, Michelle, ed. (2014) *Contemporary Approaches to Literary Trauma Theory*, Basingstoke: Palgrave Macmillan.

Bennett, Jill (2005) *Empathic Vision: Affect, Trauma, and Contemporary Art*. Stanford, CA: Stanford University Press.

Bennett, Jill and Rosanne Kennedy (2003) 'Introduction', in Jill Bennett and Rosanne Kennedy (eds), *World Memory: Personal Trajectories in Global Time*, Basingstoke: Palgrave Macmillan, pp. 1–15.

Berlant, Lauren (1997) *The Queen of America Goes to Washington City: Essays on Sex and Citizenship*, Durham, NC: Duke University Press.

Berlant, Lauren (2002) 'The Subject of True Feeling: Pain, Privacy, and Politics', in Wendy Brown and Janet Halley (eds), *Left Legalism / Left Critique*, Durham, NC: Duke University Press, pp. 105–33.

Berntsen, Dorthe and David C. Rubin (2015) 'Pretraumatic Stress Reactions in Soldiers Deployed to Afghanistan', *Clinical Psychological Science* 3.5: 63–74.

Bianchi, Bruna (2001) 'Psychiatrists, Soldiers, and Officers in Italy during the Great War', in Mark S. Micale and Paul Lerner (eds), *Traumatic Pasts: History,*

Psychiatry and Trauma in the Modern Age, 1870–1930, Cambridge: Cambridge University Press, pp. 222–52.

Blake, Linnie (2008) *The Wounds of Nations: Horror Cinema, Historical Trauma and National Identity*, Manchester: Manchester University Press.

Blanchot, Maurice (1986) *The Writing of the Disaster*, trans. Ann Smock, Lincoln, NE: University of Nebraska Press.

Blanchot, Maurice (1999) 'After the Fact', in George Quasha (ed.), *The Station Hill Blanchot Reader: Fiction and Literary Essays*, trans. Lydia Davis, Paul Auster, and Robert Lamberton, Barrytown, NY: Station Hill, pp. 487–95.

Bogacz, Ted (1989) 'War Neurosis and Cultural Change in England, 1914–1922: The Work of the War Office Committee of Enquiry into "Shell-Shock"', *Journal of Contemporary History* 24.4: 227–56.

Bond, Lucy (2011) 'Compromised Critique: A Meta-critical Analysis of American Studies after 9/11', *Journal of American Studies* 45.4: 733–56.

Bond, Lucy (2015) *Frames of Memory after 9/11: Culture, Criticism, Politics, and Law*, Basingstoke: Palgrave Macmillan.

Bradbury, Ray (1953) *Fahrenheit 451*, New York: Ballantine.

Brown, Laura S. (1995) 'Not Outside the Range: One Feminist Perspective on Psychic Trauma', in Cathy Caruth (ed.), *Trauma: Explorations in Memory*, Baltimore, MD: Johns Hopkins University Press, pp. 100–12.

Brown, Laura S. (2008) *Cultural Competence in Trauma Theory: Beyond the Flashback*, Washington, DC: American Psychological Association.

Brown, Wendy (1995) *States of Injury: Power and Freedom in Late Modernity*, Princeton, NJ: Princeton University Press.

Buelens, Gert, Sam Durrant, and Robert Eaglestone, eds (2014) *The Future of Trauma Theory: Contemporary Literary and Cultural Criticism*, Abingdon: Routledge.

Butler, Octavia (1979) *Kindred*, Boston, MA: Beacon Press.

Calhoun, Lawrence G. and Richard G. Tedeschi (1999) *Facilitating Posttraumatic Growth: A Clinician's Guide*, Mahwah, NJ: Lawrence Erlbaum Associates.

Camus, Albert (1956) *The Fall*, trans. Justin O'Brien, New York: Vintage Books.

Carey, Benedict (2018) 'Can We Really Inherit Trauma?', *New York Times* 10 December https://www.nytimes.com/2018/12/10/health/mind-epigenetics-genes.html.

Caruth, Cathy (1991) *Empirical Truths and Critical Fictions: Locke, Wordsworth, Kant, Freud*, Baltimore, MD: Johns Hopkins University Press.

Caruth, Cathy (1995a) 'Trauma and Experience: Introduction', in Cathy Caruth (ed.), *Trauma: Explorations in Memory*, Baltimore, MD: Johns Hopkins University Press, pp. 3–12.

Caruth, Cathy (1995b) 'Recapturing the Past: Introduction', in Cathy Caruth (ed.), *Trauma: Explorations in Memory*, Baltimore, MD: Johns Hopkins University Press, pp. 151–57.

Caruth, Cathy (1995c) 'Introduction: The Insistence of Reference', in Cathy Caruth and Deborah Esch (eds), *Critical Encounters: Reference and Responsibility in Deconstructive Writing*, New Brunswick, NJ: Rutgers University Press, pp. 1–8.

Caruth, Cathy (1996) *Unclaimed Experience: Trauma, Narrative, and History*, Baltimore, MD: Johns Hopkins University Press.

Caruth, Cathy (2013) *Literature in the Ashes of History*, Baltimore, MD: Johns Hopkins University Press.

Caruth, Cathy (2014) *Listening to Trauma: Conversations with Leaders in the Theory and Treatment of Catastrophic Experience*, Baltimore, MD: Johns Hopkins University Press.

Caruth, Cathy (2016) *Unclaimed Experience: Trauma, Narrative, and History*, twentieth anniversary edn, Baltimore, MD: Johns Hopkins University Press.

Caruth, Cathy and Geoffrey Hartman (1996) 'An Interview with Geoffrey Hartman', *Studies in Romanticism* 35.4: 631–52.

Césaire, Aimé (2000) *Discourse on Colonialism*, trans. Joan Pinkham, New York: Monthly Review Press.

Cesarani, David (2002) 'The Past Is Not Dead, It Is Not Even Past', *Guardian* 19 November https://www.theguardian.com/education/2002/nov/19/highereducation.race.

Cheyette, Bryan (2013) *Diasporas of the Mind: Jewish and Postcolonial Writing and the Nightmare of History*, New Haven, CT: Yale University Press.

Clarke, Richard A. (2009) 'Cheney and Rice Remember 9/11. I Do, Too', *Washington Post* 31 May http://www.washingtonpost.com/wp-dyn/content/article/2009/05/29/AR2009052901560.html.

Cox, Caroline (2001) 'Invisible Wounds: The American Legion, Shell-Shocked Veterans, and American Society, 1919–1924', in Mark S. Micale and Paul Lerner (eds), *Traumatic Pasts: History, Psychiatry and Trauma in the Modern Age, 1870–1930*, Cambridge: Cambridge University Press, pp. 280–305.

Coyle, Kevin J. and Lise Van Susteren (2012) *The Psychological Effects of Global Warming on the United States: And Why the US Mental Health Care System Is Not Adequately Prepared*, National Wildlife Federation https://nwf.org/~/media/PDFs/Global-Warming/Reports/Psych_effects_Climate_Change_Ex_Sum_3_23.ashx.

Craps, Stef (2013) *Postcolonial Witnessing: Trauma Out of Bounds*, Basingstoke: Palgrave Macmillan.

Crownshaw, Richard (2010) *The Afterlife of Holocaust Memory in Contemporary Literature and Culture*, Basingstoke: Palgrave Macmillan.

Crownshaw, Richard (2011) 'Perpetrator Fictions and Transcultural Memory', *Parallax* 17.4: 75–89.

Crownshaw, Richard, Jane Kilby, and Antony Rowland, eds (2010) *The Future of Memory*, New York: Berghahn.

Cunsolo, Ashlee and Neville R. Ellis (2018) 'Ecological Grief as a Mental Health Response to Climate Change-Related Loss', *Nature Climate Change* 8 (April): 275–81.

Cunsolo, Ashlee and Karen Landman, eds (2017) *Mourning Nature: Hope at the Heart of Ecological Loss and Grief*, Montreal and Kingston: McGill-Queen's University Press.

Davis, Walter A. (2009) 'Trauma and Tragic Transformation: Why We Learned Nothing from 9/11', in Matthew J. Morgan (ed.), *The Impact of 9/11 on Psychology and Education: The Day That Changed Everything?*, New York: Palgrave Macmillan, pp. 139–50.

Derrida, Jacques (1992) 'Canons and Metonymies: An Interview with Jacques Derrida', in Richard Rand (ed.), *Logomachia: The Contest of the Faculties*, Lincoln, NE: University of Nebraska Press, pp. 195–218.

Derrida, Jacques (1994) *Specters of Marx: The State of the Debt, the Work of Mourning, and the New International*, trans. Peggy Kamuf, New York: Routledge.

Derrida, Jacques (1995) *The Gift of Death*, trans. David Wills, Chicago, IL: University of Chicago Press.

Derrida, Jacques (1997) *The Politics of Friendship*, trans. George Collins, London: Verso.

Derrida, Jacques (1998) *Of Grammatology*, corrected edn, trans. Gayatri Chakravorty Spivak, Baltimore, MD: Johns Hopkins University Press.

Douglass, Ana and Thomas A. Vogler (2003) 'Introduction', in Ana Douglass and Thomas A. Vogler (eds), *Witness and Memory: The Discourse of Trauma*, New York: Routledge, pp. 1–53.

Duran, Edwardo *et al.* (1998) 'Healing the American Indian Soul Wound', in Yael Danieli (ed.), *International Handbook of Multigenerational Legacies of Trauma*, New York: Plenum Press, pp. 341–54.

Eaglestone, Robert (2004) *The Holocaust and the Postmodern*, Oxford: Oxford University Press.

Eaglestone, Robert (2010) 'Reading Perpetrator Testimony', in Richard Crownshaw, Jane Kilby, and Antony Rowland (eds), *The Future of Memory*, New York: Berghahn, pp. 123–134.

Eaglestone, Robert (2011) 'Avoiding Evil in Perpetrator Fiction' *Holocaust Studies* 17. 2–3: 13–26.

Edkins, Jenny (2003) *Trauma and the Memory of Politics*, Cambridge: Cambridge University Press.

Edmondson, Laura (2018) *Performing Trauma in Central Africa: Shadows of Empire*, Bloomington, IN: Indiana University Press.

Eghigian, Greg A. (2001) 'The German Welfare State as a Discourse of Trauma', in Mark S. Micale and Paul Lerner (eds), *Traumatic Pasts: History, Psychiatry and Trauma in the Modern Age, 1870–1930*, Cambridge: Cambridge University Press, pp. 92–112.

Elsaesser, Thomas (2014) *German Cinema—Terror and Trauma: Cultural Memory since 1945*, New York: Routledge.

Erichson, John (1866) *On Railway and Other Injuries of the Nervous System*, London: Walton and Maberly.

Erikson, Kai (1976) *Everything in Its Path*, New York: Simon and Schuster.

Erikson, Kai (1995) 'Notes on Trauma and Community', in Cathy Caruth (ed.), *Trauma: Explorations in Memory*, Baltimore, MD: Johns Hopkins University Press, pp. 183–99.

Eyerman, Ron (2004) 'Cultural Trauma: Slavery and the Formation of African American Identity', in Jeffrey Alexander *et al.*, *Cultural Trauma and Collective Identity*, Berkeley, CA: University of California Press, pp. 60–111.

Fanon, Frantz (1963) *The Wretched of the Earth*, trans. Constance Farrington, New York: Grove Press.

Fanon, Frantz (1967) *Black Skin, White Masks*, trans. Charles Lam Markmann, New York: Grove Press.

Farrell, Kirby (1998) *Post-traumatic Culture: Injury and Interpretation in the Nineties*, Baltimore, MD: Johns Hopkins University Press.

Fassin, Didier and Richard Rechtman (2009) *The Empire of Trauma: An Inquiry into the Condition of Victimhood*, trans. Rachel Gomme, Princeton, NJ: Princeton University Press.

Faulkner, William (1951) *Requiem for a Nun*, New York: Random House.

Felman, Shoshana (1977) 'Turning the Screw of Interpretation', *Yale French Studies* 55/56: 94–207.

Felman, Shoshana (2002) *The Juridical Unconscious: Trials and Traumas in the Twentieth Century*, Cambridge, MA: Harvard University Press.

Felman, Shoshana and Dori Laub (1992) *Testimony: Crises of Witnessing in Literature, Psychoanalysis, and History*, New York: Routledge.

Finkelstein, Norman G. (2000) *The Holocaust Industry: Reflections on the Exploitation of Jewish Suffering*, New York: Verso.

Fletcher, John (2013) *Freud and the Scene of Trauma*, New York: Fordham University Press.

Freud, Sigmund (1912) *Totem and Taboo*, in James Strachey (ed.), *The Standard Edition of the Complete Psychological Works of Sigmund Freud*, vol. 13, trans. James Strachey, Alix Strachey, and Alan Tyson, London: Hogarth Press, 1953–1974, pp. 1–161.

Freud, Sigmund (1917) 'Mourning and Melancholia', in James Strachey (ed.), *The Standard Edition of the Complete Psychological Works of Sigmund Freud*, vol. 14, trans. James Strachey, Alix Strachey, and Alan Tyson, London: Hogarth Press, 1953–1974, pp. 239–58.

Freud, Sigmund (2010a) *Beyond the Pleasure Principle*, trans. James Strachey, Seattle, WA: Pacific Publishing Studio.

Freud, Sigmund (2010b) *Moses and Monotheism*, trans. Katherine Jones, Mansfield Centre, CT: Martino Publishing.

Freud, Sigmund and Josef Breuer (1893) 'On the Psychical Mechanism of Hysterical Phenomena', in James Strachey (ed.), *The Standard Edition of the Complete Psychological Works of Sigmund Freud*, vol. 2, trans. James Strachey, Alix Strachey, and Alan Tyson, London: Hogarth Press, 1953–1974, pp. 3–17.

Freud, Sigmund and Josef Breuer (1895) *Studies on Hysteria*, in James Strachey (ed.), *The Standard Edition of the Complete Psychological Works of Sigmund Freud*, vol. 2, trans. James Strachey, Alix Strachey, and Alan Tyson, London: Hogarth Press, 1953–1974, pp. 1–335.

Fuller, Richard B. (1985) 'War Veterans' Post-traumatic Stress Disorder and the U.S. Congress', in William Kelley (ed.), *Post-traumatic Stress Disorder and the War Veteran Patient*, New York: Brunner/ Mazel, pp. 3–11.

Gibbs, Alan (2014) *Contemporary American Trauma Narratives*, Edinburgh: Edinburgh University Press.

Gilroy, Paul (1993) *The Black Atlantic: Modernity and Double Consciousness*, London: Verso.

Gilroy, Paul (2000) *Between Camps: Nations, Cultures and the Allure of Race*, London: Allen Lane.

Grayson, Hannah (2017) 'A Place for Individuals: Positive Growth in Rwanda', *Eastern African Literary and Cultural Studies*, 3.2–4: 107–30.

Grayson, Hannah (2018) 'Articulating Growth in Rwandan Terms: Adapting the Post-traumatic Growth Inventory', *Studies in Testimony* 1.1 https://studiesintestimony.co.uk/issues/volume-one-issue-one/articulating-growth-in-rwandan-terms/.

Grinker, Roy R. and John P. Spiegel (1945) *War Neuroses*, Philadelphia, PA: Blakiston.

Guerin, Frances and Roger Hallas, eds (2007) *The Image and the Witness: Trauma, Memory and Visual Culture*, London: Wallflower Press.

Haberman, Clyde (2009) 'A Trauma That Rippled Outward', *New York Times* 10 September https://www.nytimes.com/2009/09/11/nyregion/11nyc.html.

Hamilton, Carrie (2010) 'Activist Memories: The Politics of Trauma and the Pleasures of Politics', in Richard Crownshaw, Jane Kilby, and Antony Rowland (eds), *The Future of Memory*, New York: Berghahn, pp. 265–78.

Harpham, Geoffrey Galt (1999) *Shadows of Ethics: Criticism and the Just Society*, Durham, NC: Duke University Press.

Harrington, Ralph (2001) 'The Railway Accident: Trains, Trauma, and Technological Crises in Nineteenth-Century Britain', in Mark S. Micale and Paul Lerner (eds), *Traumatic Pasts: History, Psychiatry and Trauma in the Modern Age, 1870–1930*, Cambridge: Cambridge University Press, pp. 31–56.

Hartman, Geoffrey H. (1964) *Wordsworth's Poetry, 1787–1814*, New Haven, CT: Yale University Press.

Hartman, Geoffrey H. (1980) *Criticism in the Wilderness: The Study of Literature Today*, New Haven, CT: Yale University Press.

Hartman, Geoffrey H. (1981) *Saving the Text: Literature/Derrida/Philosophy*, Baltimore, MD: Johns Hopkins University Press.

Hartman, Geoffrey H. (1995) 'On Traumatic Knowledge and Literary Studies', *New Literary History* 26.3: 537–63.

Hartman, Geoffrey H. (1996) *The Longest Shadow: In the Aftermath of the Holocaust*, Bloomington, IN: Indiana University Press.

Hartman, Geoffrey H. (1997) *The Fateful Question of Culture*, New York: Columbia University Press.

Hartman, Geoffrey H. (1998) 'Shoah and Intellectual Witness', *Partisan Review* 65.1: 37–48.

Hartman, Geoffrey H. (2000) 'Memory.com: Tele-suffering and Testimony in the Dot Com Era', *Raritan* 19.3:1–18.

Hartman, Geoffrey H. (2006) 'The Humanities of Testimony: An Introduction', *Poetics Today* 27.2: 249–60.

Hartman, Geoffrey H. (2007) *A Scholar's Tale: Intellectual Journey of a Displaced Child of Europe*, New York: Fordham University Press.

Herman, Judith L. (1992a) 'Complex PTSD: A Syndrome in Survivors of Prolonged and Repeated Trauma', *Journal of Traumatic Stress* 5.3: 377–91.

Herman, Judith L (1992b) *Trauma and Recovery: The Aftermath of Violence—from Domestic Abuse to Political Terror*, New York: Basic Books.

Hirsch, Joshua (2004) *Afterimage: Film, Trauma, and the Holocaust*, Philadelphia, PA: Temple University Press.

Hirsch, Marianne (1992) 'Family Pictures: Maus, Mourning, and Post-Memory', *Discourse* 15.2: 3–29.

Hirsch, Marianne (1997) *Family Frames: Photography, Narrative, and Postmemory*, Cambridge, MA: Harvard University Press.

Hirsch, Marianne (2001) 'Surviving Images: Holocaust Photographs and the Work of Postmemory', *Yale Journal of Criticism* 14.1: 5–38.

Hirsch, Marianne (2008) 'The Generation of Postmemory', *Poetics Today* 29.1: 103–28.

Hirsch, Marianne (2012) *The Generation of Postmemory: Writing and Visual Culture after the Holocaust*, New York: Columbia University Press.

Hoffman, Eva (2004) *After Such Knowledge: Memory, History, and the Legacy of the Holocaust*, New York: Public Affairs.

Hungerford, Amy (2003) *The Holocaust of Texts: Genocide, Literature, and Personification*, Chicago, IL: Chicago University Press.

Janet, Pierre (1894) 'Histoire d'une idée fixe', *Revue Philosophique* 37.1: 121–63.

Janet, Pierre (1898) *Névroses et idées fixes*, vol. 1, Paris: Félix Alcan.

Janoff-Bulman, Ronnie (1992) *Shattered Assumptions: Towards a New Psychology of Trauma*, New York: Free Press.

Kansteiner, Wulf and Harald Weilnböck (2008) 'Against the Concept of Cultural Trauma Theory (or How I Learned to Love the Suffering of Others without the Help of Psychotherapy)', in Astrid Erll and Ansgar Nünning (eds), *Cultural Memory Studies: An International and Interdisciplinary Handbook*, Berlin: Walter de Gruyter, pp. 229–40.

Kaplan, E. Ann (2005) *Trauma Culture: The Politics of Terror and Loss in Media and Literature*, New Brunswick, NJ: Rutgers University Press.

Kaplan, E. Ann (2013) 'Trauma Studies Moving Forward: Interdisciplinary Perspectives', *Journal of Dramatic Theory and Criticism* 27.2: 53–65.

Kaplan, E. Ann (2016) *Climate Trauma: Foreseeing the Future in Dystopian Film and Fiction*, New Brunswick, NJ: Rutgers University Press.

Kaplan, E. Ann and Ban Wang, eds (2004) *Trauma and Cinema: Cross-Cultural Explorations*, Hong Kong: Hong Kong University Press.

Kardiner, Abram (1941) *The Traumatic Neuroses of War*, Washington, DC: National Research Council.

Kennedy, Rosanne and Tikka Jan Wilson (2003) 'Constructing Shared Histories: Stolen Generations Testimony, Narrative Therapy and Address', in Jill

Bennett and Rosanne Kennedy (eds), *World Memory: Personal Trajectories in Global Time*, Basingstoke: Palgrave Macmillan, pp. 119–39.
Kilby, Jane (2010) 'The Future of Trauma: Introduction', in Richard Crownshaw, Jane Kilby, and Antony Rowland (eds), *The Future of Memory*, New York: Berghahn, pp. 181–90.
Kushner, Howard I. (2009) *A Cursing Brain? The Histories of Tourette Syndrome*, Cambridge, MA: Harvard University Press.
LaCapra, Dominick (1994) *Representing the Holocaust: History, Theory, Trauma*, Ithaca, NY: Cornell University Press.
LaCapra, Dominick (1998) *History and Memory after Auschwitz*, Baltimore, MD: Johns Hopkins University Press.
LaCapra, Dominick (2001) *Writing History, Writing Trauma*, Baltimore, MD: Johns Hopkins University Press.
LaCapra, Dominick (2004) *History in Transit: Experience, Identity, Critical Theory*, Ithaca, NY: Cornell University Press.
LaCapra, Dominick (2009) *History and Its Limits: Human, Animal, Violence*, Ithaca, NY: Cornell University Press.
LaCapra, Dominick (2014) *Writing History, Writing Trauma*, second edn, Baltimore, MD: Johns Hopkins University Press.
LaCapra, Dominick (2018) *Understanding Others: Peoples, Animals, Pasts*, Ithaca, NY: Cornell University Press.
Lambek, Michael and Paul Antze (1996) 'Introduction: Forecasting Memory', in Paul Antze and Michael Lambek (eds), *Tense Past: Cultural Essays in Trauma and Memory*, London: Routledge, pp. xi–xxxviii.
Landsberg, Alison (2004) *Prosthetic Memory: The Transformation of American Remembrance in the Age of Mass Culture*, New York: Columbia University Press.
Lerner, Paul (2001) 'From Traumatic Neurosis to Male Hysteria: The Decline and Fall of Hermann Oppenheim', in Mark S. Micale and Paul Lerner (eds), *Traumatic Pasts: History, Psychiatry and Trauma in the Modern Age, 1870–1930*, Cambridge: Cambridge University Press, pp. 140–71.
Levi, Primo (1989) 'The Grey Zone', in *The Drowned and the Saved*, trans. Raymond Rosenthal, London: Abacus, pp. 22–51.
Leys, Ruth (2000) *Trauma: A Genealogy*, Chicago, IL: University of Chicago Press.
Lifton, Robert Jay (1967) *Death in Life: Survivors of Hiroshima*, New York: Random House.
Lifton, Robert Jay (1973) *Home from the War: Vietnam Veterans Neither Victims Nor Executioners*, New York: Simon and Schuster.
Litz, Brett T., *et al.* (2009) 'Moral Injury and Moral Repair in War Veterans: A Preliminary Model and Intervention Strategy', *Clinical Psychology Review* 29.8: 695–706.
Lowenstein, Adam (2005) *Shocking Representation: Historical Trauma, National Cinema, and the Modern Horror Film*, New York: Columbia University Press.
Luckhurst, Roger (2003) 'Trauma Culture', *New Formations* 50.3: 28–47.

Luckhurst, Roger (2008) *The Trauma Question*, London: Routledge.

Lyotard, Jean-François (1984) *The Postmodern Condition: A Report on Knowledge*, trans. Geoff Bennington and Brian Massumi, Minneapolis, MN: University of Minnesota Press.

Lyotard, Jean-François (1988) *The Differend: Phrases in Dispute*, trans. Georges Van Den Abbeele, Manchester: Manchester University Press.

Lyotard, Jean-François (1993) *The Postmodern Explained: Correspondence, 1982–1985*, ed. Julian Pefanis and Morgan Thomas, trans. Don Barry, Minneapolis, MN: University of Minnesota Press.

MacNair, Rachel M. (2002) *Perpetration-Induced Traumatic Stress: The Psychological Consequences of Killing*, Westport, CT: Praeger.

Mays, Jeffery C. (2018) 'Prominent Lawyer in Fight for Gay Rights Dies after Setting Himself on Fire in Prospect Park', *New York Times* 14 April https://www.nytimes.com/2018/04/14/nyregion/david-buckel-dead-fire.html.

McGlothlin, Erin (2010) 'Theorizing the Perpetrator in Bernhard Schlink's *The Reader* and Martin Amis's *Time's Arrow*', in R. Clifton Spargo and Robert M. Ehrenreich (eds), *After Representation? The Holocaust, Literature, and Culture*, New Brunswick, NJ: Rutgers University Press, pp. 210–30.

McGlothlin, Erin (2014) 'Narrative Perspective and the Holocaust Perpetrator: Edgar Hilsenrath's *The Nazi and the Barber* and Jonathan Littell's *The Kindly Ones*', in Jenni Adams (ed.), *The Bloomsbury Companion to Holocaust Literature*, London: Bloomsbury.

McGlothlin, Erin (2016) 'Empathetic Identification and the Mind of the Holocaust Perpetrator in Fiction: A Proposed Taxonomy of Response', *Narrative* 24.3: 251–76.

Meek, Allen (2009) *Trauma and Media: Theories, Histories, and Images*, New York: Routledge.

Micale, Mark S. (2001) 'Jean-Martin Charcot and *les névroses traumatiques*: From Medicine to Culture in French Trauma Theory of the Late Nineteenth Century', in Mark S. Micale and Paul Lerner (eds), *Traumatic Pasts: History, Psychiatry and Trauma in the Modern Age, 1870–1930*, Cambridge: Cambridge University Press, pp. 115–39.

Micale, Mark S. and Paul Lerner (2001) 'Trauma, Psychiatry, and History: A Conceptual and Historiographical Introduction', in Mark S. Micale and Paul Lerner (eds), *Traumatic Pasts: History, Psychiatry and Trauma in the Modern Age, 1870–1930*, Cambridge: Cambridge University Press, pp. 1–27.

Morag, Raya (2013) *Waltzing with Bashir: Perpetrator Trauma and Cinema*, London: I. B. Tauris.

Morrison, Toni (1987) *Beloved*, London: Chatto and Windus.

Morrison, Toni (1992). *Jazz*, New York: Alfred J. Knopf.

Mowitt, John (2000) 'Trauma Envy', *Cultural Critique* 46.3: 272–97.

Neal, Arthur G. (2005) *National Trauma and Collective Memory: Extraordinary Events in the American Experience*, second edn, London: M. E. Sharpe.

Nussbaum, Martha C. (1990) *Love's Knowledge: Essays on Philosophy and Literature*, Oxford: Oxford University Press.

Nussbaum, Martha C. (1995) *Poetic Justice: The Literary Imagination and Public Life*, Boston, MA: Beacon Press.

Obama, Barack (2008) 'A More Perfect Union', National Constitution Center 18 March https://constitutioncenter.org/amoreperfectunion/docs/Race_Speech_Tra nscript.pdf.

Oberhaus, Daniel (2017) 'Climate Change Is Giving Us "Pre-traumatic Stress"', Motherboard 4 February https://motherboard.vice.com /en_us/article/vvzzam/ climate-change-is-giving-us-pre-traumatic-stress.

Oppenheim, Hermann (1889) *Die traumatischen Neurosen nach den in der Nervenklinik der Charité in den 5 Jahren 1883–1888 gesammelten Beobachtungen*, Berlin: Hirschwald.

Page, Herbert W. (1883) *Injuries of the Spine and Spinal Cord without Apparent Mechanical Lesion and Nervous Shock, in Their Surgical and Medico-Legal Aspects*, London: J. and A. Churchill.

Page, Herbert W. (1891) *Railway Injuries: With Special Reference to Those of the Back and Nervous System, in Their Medico-Legal and Clinical Aspects*, London: Charles Griffon and Co.

Panero, James (2014) 'Grounded Zero', *New Criterion* September https://www.new criterion.com/issues/2014/9/grounded-zero.

Parker, David (1998) 'Introduction: The Turn to Ethics in the 1990s', in Jane Adamson, Richard Freadman, and David Parker (eds), *Renegotiating Ethics in Literature, Philosophy, and Theory*, Cambridge: Cambridge University Press, pp. 1–17.

Pease, Donald E. (2009) *The New American Exceptionalism*, Minneapolis, MN: University of Minnesota Press.

Pederson, Joshua (forthcoming) *Sin Sick: Moral Injury in Literature*.

Plunka, Gene A. (2018) *Holocaust Theater: Dramatizing Survivor Testimony and Its Effects on the Second Generation*, Abingdon: Routledge.

Press, Eyal (2018) 'The Wounds of the Drone Warrior', *New York Times Magazine* 13 June https://www.nytimes.com/2018/06/13/magazine/veterans-ptsd-drone-wa rrior-wounds.html.

Radstone, Susannah (2001) 'Social Bonds and Psychical Order: Testimonies', *Cultural Values* 5.1: 59–78.

Radstone, Susannah (2007a) 'Theory and Affect: Undivided Worlds', in Perri 6 *et al.* (eds), *Public Emotions*, Basingstoke: Palgrave Macmillan, pp. 181–201.

Radstone, Susannah (2007b) 'Trauma Theory: Contexts, Politics, Ethics', *Paragraph: A Journal of Modern Critical Theory* 30.1: 9–29.

Rafferty, Terrence (1993) 'A Man of Transactions', *New Yorker* 20 December: 129–32.

Rankine, Claudia (2014) *Citizen: An American Lyric*, Minneapolis, MN: Graywolf.

Rastegar, Kamran (2015) *Surviving Images: Cinema, War, and Cultural Memory in the Middle East*, New York: Oxford University Press.

Reading, Anna and Tamar Katriel (2015) 'Introduction', in Anna Reading and Tamar Katriel (eds), *Cultural Memories of Nonviolent Struggles: Powerful Times*, Basingstoke: Palgrave Macmillan, pp. 1–31.

'Report: More US Soldiers Suffering from Pre-traumatic Stress Disorder' (2006) *Onion* 15 November http://www.theonion.com/articles/report-more-us-soldiers-suffer ingfrom-pretraumati,2088/.

Richardson, John H. (2015) 'When the End of Human Civilization Is Your Day Job', *Esquire* August https://www.esquire.com/news-politics/a36228/ballad-of-the-sad-climatol ogists-0815/.

Rigney, Ann (2018) 'Remembering Hope: Transnational Activism beyond the Traumatic', *Memory Studies* 11.3: 368–80.

Robbins, Bruce (2017) *The Beneficiary*, Durham, NC: Duke University Press.

Romero-Jódar, Andrés (2017) *The Trauma Graphic Novel*, New York: Routledge.

Root, Maria P. P. (1992) 'Reconstructing the Impact of Trauma on Personality', in Laura S. Brown and Mary Ballou (eds), *Personality and Psychopathology: Feminist Reappraisals*, New York: Guilford Press, pp. 229–65.

Ross, Brian and Rehab El-Buri (2008) 'Obama's Pastor: God Damn America, U.S. to Blame for 9/11', *ABC News* 13 March https://abcnews.go.com/Blotter/Dem ocraticDebate/story?id=4443788&page=1.

Rothberg, Michael (2000) *Traumatic Realism: The Demands of Holocaust Representation*, Minneapolis, MN: University of Minnesota Press.

Rothberg, Michael (2009) *Multidirectional Memory: Remembering the Holocaust in the Age of Decolonization*. Stanford, CA: Stanford University Press.

Rothberg, Michael (2011) 'From Gaza to Warsaw: Mapping Multidirectional Memory', *Criticism: A Quarterly for Literature and the Arts* 53.4: 523–48.

Rothberg, Michael (2014a) 'Beyond Tancred and Clorinda: Trauma Studies for Implicated Subjects', in Gert Buelens, Sam Durrant, and Robert Eaglestone (eds), *The Future of Trauma Theory: Contemporary Literary and Cultural Criticism*, Abingdon: Routledge, pp. xi–xviii.

Rothberg, Michael (2014b) 'Trauma Theory, Implicated Subjects, and the Question of Israel/Palestine', *Profession* https://profession.mla.org/trauma-theory-imp licated-subjects-and-the-question-of-israel-palestine/.

Rothe, Anne (2011) *Popular Media Culture: Selling the Pain of Others in the Mass Media*, New Brunswick, NJ: Rutgers University Press.

Rothe, Anne (2016) 'Irresponsible Nonsense: An Epistemological and Ethical Critique of Postmodern Trauma Theory', in Yochai Ataria *et al.* (eds), *Interdisciplinary Handbook of Trauma and Culture*, New York: Springer, pp. 181–94.

Roudebush, Marc (2001) 'A Battle of Nerves: Hysteria and Its Treatments in France during World War I', in Mark S. Micale and Paul Lerner (eds), *Traumatic Pasts: History, Psychiatry and Trauma in the Modern Age, 1870–1930*, Cambridge: Cambridge University Press, pp. 253–79.

Rowland, Antony (1997) 'Re-reading "Impossibility" and "Barbarism": Adorno and Post-Holocaust Poetics', *Critical Survey* 9.1: 57–69.

Saint-Amour, Paul K. (2015a) *Tense Future: Modernism, Total War, Encyclopedic Form*, Oxford: Oxford University Press.

Saint-Amour, Paul K. (2015b) 'Waiting for the Bomb to Drop', *New York Times* 3 August https://opinionator.blogs.nytimes.com/author/paul-saint-amour/.

Saltzman, Lisa and Eric Rosenberg (2006) *Trauma and Visuality in Modernity*, Hanover, NH: Dartmouth College Press / University Press of New England.

Sanyal, Debarati (2015) *Memory and Complicity: Migrations of Holocaust Remembrance*, New York: Fordham University Press.

Seltzer, Mark (1997) 'Wound Culture', *October* 80.1: 3–26.

Seltzer, Mark (1998) *Serial Killers: Death and Life in America's Wound Culture*, London: Routledge.

Shatan, Chaim F. (1972) 'Post-Vietnam Syndrome', *New York Times* 6 May https://www.nytimes.com/1972/05/06/archives/postvietnam-syndrome.html.

Shay, Jonathan (1995) *Achilles in Vietnam: Combat Trauma and the Undoing of Character*, New York: Scribner.

Sicher, Efraim (2000) 'The Future of the Past: Countermemory and Postmemory in Contemporary American Post-Holocaust Narratives', *History & Memory* 12.2: 56–91.

Silverman, Max (2013) *Palimpsestic Memory: The Holocaust and Colonialism in French and Francophone Fiction and Film*, New York: Berghahn.

Smelser, Neil J. (2004) 'Psychological Trauma and Cultural Trauma', in Jeffrey Alexander *et al.*, *Cultural Trauma and Collective Identity*, Berkeley, CA: University of California Press, pp. 31–59.

Smethurst, Tobi (2015) 'Playing Dead in Video Games: Trauma in *Limbo*', *Journal of Popular Culture* 48.5: 817–35.

Smethurst, Tobi (2017) '"We Put Our Hands on the Trigger with Him": Guilt and Perpetration in *Spec Ops: The Line*', *Criticism: A Quarterly for Literature and the Arts* 59.2: 201–21.

Smethurst, Toby and Stef Craps (2015) 'Playing with Trauma: Interreactivity, Empathy, and Complicity in *The Walking Dead* Video Game', *Games and Culture* 10.3: 269–90.

Sontag, Susan (2003) *Regarding the Pain of Others*, New York: Farrar, Straus, and Giroux.

Spanierman, Lisa B. and V. Paul Poteat (2005) 'Moving beyond Complacency to Commitment: Multicultural Research in Counseling Psychology', *Counseling Psychologist* 33.4: 513–23.

Spiegelman, Art (1986) *Maus: A Survivor's Tale: My Father Bleeds History*, New York: Pantheon Books.

Spiegelman, Art (1991) *Maus II: A Survivor's Tale: And Here My Troubles Began*, New York: Pantheon Books.

Steiner, George (1967) *Language and Silence: Essays on Language, Literature, and the Inhuman*, New York: Atheneum.

Stocks, Claire (2007) 'Trauma Theory and the Singular Self: Rethinking Extreme Experiences in the Light of Cross-Cultural Identity', *Textual Practice* 21.1: 71–92.

Summerfield, Derek (1999) 'A Critique of Seven Assumptions behind Psychological Trauma Programmes in War-Affected Areas', *Social Science and Medicine* 48: 1449–62.

Summerfield, Derek (2004) 'Cross-Cultural Perspectives on the Medicalization of Human Suffering', in Gerald M. Rosen (ed.), *Posttraumatic Stress Disorder: Issues and Controversies*, Chichester: Wiley, pp. 233–45.

Tal, Kalí (1996) *Worlds of Hurt: Reading the Literatures of Trauma*, Cambridge: Cambridge University Press.

Tan, Siang Y. and Daito Shigaki (2007) 'Jean-Martin Charcot (1825–1893): Pathologist Who Shaped Modern Neurology', *Singapore Medical Journal* 48.5: pp. 383–84.

Terr, Lenore C. (1991) 'Childhood Traumas: An Outline and Overview', *American Journal of Psychiatry* 148.1: 10–20.

Thomas, Madeleine (2014) 'Climate Depression Is for Real: Just Ask a Scientist', *Grist* 28 October https://grist.org/climate-energy/climate-depression-is-for-real-just-ask-a-scientist/.

Tobi, Elmar W. *et al.* (2018) 'DNA Methylation as a Mediator of the Association between Prenatal Adversity and Risk Factors for Metabolic Disease in Adulthood', *Science Advances* 4.1 http://advances.sciencemag.org/content/4/1/eaao4364.

Tomsky, Terri (2011) 'From Sarajevo to 9/11: Travelling Memory and the Trauma Economy', *Parallax* 17.4: 49–60.

'Trauma' (2009) *Oxford English Dictionary*, second edn, Oxford: Oxford University Press, CD-ROM.

Trimarco, James and Molly Hurley Depret (2005) 'Wounded Nation, Broken Time', in Dana Heller (ed.), *The Selling of 9/11: How a National Tragedy Became a Commodity*, New York: Palgrave Macmillan, pp. 27–53.

van Alphen, Ernst (1997) *Caught by History: Holocaust Effects in Contemporary Art, Literature, and Theory*, Stanford, CA: Stanford University Press.

van der Hart, Onno, Paul Brown, and Bessel A. van der Kolk (1989) 'Pierre Janet's Treatment of Post-traumatic Stress', *Journal of Traumatic Stress* 2.4: 379–95.

van der Hart, Onno and Barbara Friedman (1989) 'A Reader's Guide to Pierre Janet: A Neglected Intellectual Heritage', *Dissociation* 2.1: 3–16.

van der Hart, Onno and Rutger Horst (1989) 'The Dissociation Theory of Pierre Janet', *Journal of Traumatic Stress* 2.4: 397–412.

Van Susteren, Lise (2017) 'A Closer Look—Our Moral Obligation: The Duty to Warn and Act', in Susan Clayton *et al.* (eds), *Mental Health and Our Changing Climate: Impacts, Implications, and Guidance*, Washington, DC: American Psychological Association / ecoAmerica, p. 57.

Vermeulen, Pieter (2010) *Geoffrey Hartman: Romanticism after the Holocaust*, London: Continuum.

Vermeulen, Pieter (2011) 'Video Testimony, Modernity, and the Claims of Melancholia', *Criticism: A Quarterly for Literature and the Arts* 53.4: 549–68.

Vice, Sue (2013) 'Exploring the Fictions of Perpetrator Suffering', *Journal of Literature and Trauma Studies* 2.1–2: 15–25.

Vickroy, Laurie (2002) *Trauma and Survival in Contemporary Fiction*, Charlottesville, VA: University of Virginia Press.

Walker, Janet (2005) *Trauma Cinema: Documenting Incest and the Holocaust*, Berkeley, CA: University of California Press.
War Office Committee (2014) *Report of the War Office Committee into the Condition of Shellshock*, Uckfield, E. Sussex: Naval and Military Press.
Watters, Ethan (2010) *Crazy like Us: The Globalization of the American Psyche*, New York: Free Press.
Weissman, Gary (1995) 'A Fantasy of Witnessing', *Media, Culture & Society* 17.2: 293–307.
Weissman, Gary (2004) *Fantasies of Witnessing: Postwar Efforts to Experience the Holocaust*, Ithaca, NY: Cornell University Press.
Whitehead, Anne (2004) *Trauma Fiction*, Edinburgh: Edinburgh University Press.
Wiesel, Elie (1960) *Night*, trans. Stella Rodway, New York: Hill and Wang.
Wilkomirski, Binjamin (1996) *Fragments: Memories of a Wartime Childhood*, trans. Carol Brown Janeway, New York: Schocken.
Williamson Sinalo, Caroline (2018) *Rwanda after Genocide: Gender, Identity and Post-traumatic Growth*, Cambridge: Cambridge University Press.
Wolmar, Christian (2007) *Fire & Steam: A New History of the Railways in Britain*, London: Atlantic Books.
Young, Allan (1995) *The Harmony of Illusions: Inventing Post-traumatic Stress Disorder*, Princeton, NJ: Princeton University Press.
Zimmer, Carl (2018) 'The Famine Ended 70 Years Ago, but Dutch Genes Still Bear Scars', *New York Times*31 Januaryhttps://www.nytimes.com/2018/01/31/science/dutch-famine-genes.html.

Index

Abani, Chris, 125
absence, 79, 81
Achilles in Vietnam (Shay), 122
acting-out, 74–79
Act of Killing, The (Oppenheimer), 122
ACT UP, 141
Adorno, Theodor, 7, 45–46, 50, 72, 112
Afghanistan War, 99, 123, 126–27
Afterwards (Seiffert), 122
AIDS epidemic, 43
Alexander, Jeffrey, 100–01
Allah Is Not Obliged (Kourouma), 125
al-Qaeda, 123
American Legion, 32
American Psychiatric Association (APA), 7, 35–41
American Psychological Association (APA), 89
Amis, Martin, 121–22, 125
anticipatory anxiety. *See* anxiety
anti-Semitism, 27, 52
Antze, Paul, 137
anxiety, 35, 56, 126–30
apartheid, 104–05
Arendt, Hannah, 110, 121
Attridge, Derek, 54
Auschwitz, 3, 7, 45–50, 76, 84, 112

Babinski, Joseph, 19, 29
Ball, Karyn, 135
Barker, Pat, 6
Barthes, Roland, 84
Baudrillard, Jean, 135
Beah, Ishmael, 125
bearing witness, 50, 55, 59–60, 65–72, 75, 82–83, 87–94, 115
Beasts of No Nation (Iweala), 125
Beckett, Samuel, 48
Beloved (Morrison), 5, 56, 83
Benigni, Roberto, 125
Benjamin, Walter, 71
Bennet, Jill, 113
Berlant, Lauren, 42, 139–40
Berntsen, Dorthe, 126
Between Camps (Gilroy), 110
Beyond the Pleasure Principle (Freud), 23–24, 26, 32, 57, 127
Black Atlantic, The (Gilroy), 110
Black Lives Matter, 3, 141
Black Skin, White Masks (Fanon), 109
Blake, William, 63
Blanchard's Physical Dictionary, 2
Blanchot, Maurice, 7, 48, 50, 72
Bloom, Harold, 51
Bogacz, Ted, 31
Bond, Lucy, 80, 116
Box, Jason, 130
Bradbury, Ray, 92
Breuer, Josef, 23–24
Bricmont, Jean, 135
Brown, Laura, 40, 107
Brown, Wendy, 139–40
Browning, Christopher, 121
Buckel, David, 130
Buffalo Creek flood, 98
Bush, George, 99–100
Butler, Octavia, 88–89
bystanders, 82, 134

Calhoun, Lawrence, 137
Camus, Albert, 67–68, 76
Carey, Benedict, 87
Caruth, Cathy: critiques of, 96–97, 115, 117; and Sigmund Freud, 24, 27–28; works of, 7–8, 51–61, 63–64, 74–77, 79–80, 93, 106, 132–34
catalysing event, 25, 37, 39
Celan, Paul, 48, 67–68

Césaire, Aimé, 110
Cesarani, David, 10
Charcot, Jean-Martin, 7, 19–21, 31
Cheyette, Bryan, 111
child soldiers, 125
Citizen: An American Lyric (Rankine), 105
Civil War, the, 86
Clarke, Richard, 99
classism, 108
climate change, 2, 11, 43, 128–31, 141–42
Climate Trauma (Kaplan), 128–29
Clinton, Bill, 99–100
closure, 54, 60, 71
Cold War, the, 42, 128
Coleridge, Samuel Taylor, 63
collective trauma, 8, 27, 94–102
colonialism, 41, 104–12
combat fatigue, 14
community of trauma, 98
compensation claims, 15–18, 29, 36
complex post-traumatic stress disorder, 40, 109
concentration camps, 3, 56, 84, 124. *See also* Holocaust, the
consciousness, 4, 22–26, 57–58, 63–64
Contemporary American Trauma Narratives (Gibbs), 103, 116, 121
Contemporary Approaches in Literary Trauma Theory, 103
coping mechanisms, 34
Cox, Caroline, 32
Craps, Stef, 106, 135
crisis of listening, 75, 80
crisis of literature, 75
crisis of representation, 114
crisis of witnessing, 65–72
Critical Encounters (Caruth), 51
Criticism in the Wilderness (Hartman), 62
Crownshaw, Richard, 4, 98, 121, 123
cultural materialism, 8, 51
cultural studies, 8, 51, 121
cultural trauma, 101–02
cultural trauma theory, 10, 73, 93–94, 102, 123–24
Cunsolo, Ashlee, 130
Davis, Walter, 100
deconstruction, 7–8, 50–52, 54–55, 60–62, 66, 72, 135
de Graef, Ortwin, 52
Deleuze, Giles, 135
de Man, Paul, 51–53, 55, 59, 62, 67, 93
de Man affair, the, 51–53
DeMille, Cecil B., 88
Demjanjuk, John, 117
denial, 78
departure from trauma, 80–81
Depret, Molly Hurley, 100
Derrida, Jacques, 51, 54–55, 61–62, 66, 93
de Saussure, Ferdinand, 50
diagnosis of trauma, 28–33, 35–41, 122
Diagnostic and Statistical Manual of Mental Disorders (DSM), 7, 35–51, 55–56, 108, 119
Diasporas of the Mind (Cheyette), 111
differend, 49–50
Differend: Phrases in Dispute, The (Lyotard), 49–50
Discourse on Colonialism (Césaire), 110
discrimination, 41, 105
disorders of extreme stress not otherwise specified, 109
dissociation, 20–21
domestic violence, 39–40
Donaghue, Phil, 114
Dongala, Emmanuel, 125
Dostoevsky, Fyodor, 68
Douglass, Ana, 53
dreams, 20, 22, 37, 56–58, 127
drug abuse, 34
Duggan, Mark, 105
Dutch Hunger Winter, 86

Eaglestone, Robert, 54, 121
echo-chamber effect, 116
ecological grief, 130–31
Eghigian, Greg, 17
Eichmann, Adolf, 70
Eisenman, Peter, 3
Ellis, Neville, 130
empathetic listener, 69

empathy, 69, 82, 91
Empire of Trauma, The (Fassin and Rechtman), 119
Empirical Truths and Critical Fictions (Caruth), 55
epigenetics, 86–87
Erichsen, John, 14–15
Erikson, Kai, 74, 98–99
Eurocentrism, 104
European Romanticism, 61–62
Eyerman, Ron, 100–01

Fahrenheit 451 (Bradbury), 92
Fall, The (Camus), 76
Family Frames (Hirsch), 83–84
Fanon, Frantz, 109
fantasies of witnessing, 90–91
Farrell, Kirby, 42–43
Fashionable Nonsense (Sokal and Bricmont), 135
Fassin, Didier, 119–20
Fateful Question of Culture, The (Hartman), 64
Faulkner, William, 1–2, 10
Felman, Shoshana, 7–8, 52, 55, 59, 65–72, 75, 83, 93, 106, 115, 117
feminism, 3, 8, 39, 41
Finkelstein, Norman, 90–91
First World, 110
First World War, 2, 7, 26–33, 41, 57, 128
fixed idea. *See idée fixe*
Fletcher, John, 24
Folman, Ari, 122
Ford, Ford Madox, 128
Fortunoff Video Archive for Holocaust Testimonies, 55, 65–66, 68–69
fragmentation, 112
Fragments (Wilkormirski), 92
Freud, Sigmund: anxiety and, 127; Caruth and, 57–60; collective trauma and, 94–97, 118; hysteria and, 14, 19, 21, 23–27; LaCapra and, 78–79; model of trauma and, 4, 7, 38; warfare and trauma and, 32
Friedlander, Saul, 76
fright, 20
Future of Memory, The, 103, 104
Future of Trauma Theory, The, 103, 141

gay rights activism, 3
gender, 20, 107
Generation of Postmemory, The (Hirsch), 86
genocide, 56, 62, 92
Geoffrey Hartman: Romanticism after the Holocaust (Vermeulen), 62
German welfare state, 16
Germany Imperial Insurance Office, 18
Gibbs, Alan, 103, 116, 120–21, 123
Gift of Death, The (Derrida), 54
Gilroy, Paul, 110
globalization, 104
Goldhagen, Daniel, 121
grand narratives, 49
Great Depression, the, 42, 99
grey zone, 124–25
Grey Zone, The (Nelson), 125
Grinker, Roy, 33
Guantánamo Bay, 99
Gulf War Syndrome, 14

Hamilton, Carrie, 137, 139
Harpham, Geoffrey, 54
Harrington, Ralph, 15
Hartman, Geoffrey, 7–8, 51–52, 55, 59, 61–65, 106, 117, 135
Heijmans, Bas, 86
heredity, 20–21, 29–30, 86
Herman, Judith, 5, 21, 39–40
heterosexism, 108
Hilberg, Raul, 121
Hiroshima, 33
Hiroshima mon amour (Resnais), 115
Hirsch, Marianne, 83–86
historical trauma, 79–83
Hitler, Adolf, 10
Hoche, Alfred, 19
Hoffman, Eva, 86
Holocaust, the: industry of, 90; legacy of, 3, 9–10, 84–85, 88, 104, 110–12, 139;

perpetrators of, 121–22; portrayal of, 125; testimonies of, 55, 65–70, 106, 117, 124; and the trauma canon, 112–16; writing about, 45–50, 54, 76, 86
Holocaust of Texts, The (Hungerford), 92
Holthaus, Eric, 130
Home from the War (Lifton), 33–34
House and Senate Veterans Affairs Committees, 35–36, 39
Hungerford, Amy, 83, 92
Huyssen, Andreas, 139
hypnosis, 20, 22–23
hysteria, 7, 13, 18–31

idée fixe, 22
Illiad, The (Homer), 122
immigration, 88
implicated subject, 124, 142
indigenous writing, 113
industrialization, 12–19, 64, 106
insidious trauma, 109
Iraq War, 99, 123
Iweala, Uzodinma, 125

James, Henry, 66
Janet, Pierre, 7, 19, 21–23, 25, 58
Jarrett-Macauley, Delia, 125
Jazz (Morrison), 5
Johnny Mad Dog (Dongala), 125
Joyce, James, 128
Judaism, 95–96
Juridical Unconscious, The (Felman), 70

Kansteiner, Wulf, 132–34, 136
Kaplan, E. Ann, 74, 89–90, 94, 128–30
Karadzic, Radovan, 117
Kardiner, Abram, 32
Katriel, Tamar, 138–39
Keats, John, 63
Kellner, Tatana, 86
Kennedy, Rosanne, 113
Kilby, Jane, 104
Kindly Ones, The (Littell), 122
Kindred (Butler), 88
King, Stephen, 114
Korean War, 42
Kourouma, Ahmadou, 125
Kraepelin, Emil, 38
Kreutzer Sonata, The (Tolstoy), 71
Kristeva, Julia, 135

Lacan, Jacques, 135
LaCapra, Dominick, 8, 76–77, 93, 106, 110, 118, 135
Lake, Ricki, 114
Lambek, Michael, 137
Landsberg, Alison, 74, 88–89, 94
Langer, Lawrence, 117
Lanzmann, Claude, 67, 76, 125
'Last Days of Muhammad Atta, The' (Amis), 122
Last of the Unjust, The (Lanzmann), 125
latency, 27, 56–58, 95–97
Laub, Dori, 8, 55, 65–72, 75–76, 80, 83, 106, 117
Lerner, Paul, 5, 13, 28–29
Levi, Primo, 124
Levinas, Emmanuel, 54
Levinthal, David, 86
Leys, Ruth, 5, 27, 83, 118, 132–33, 136
Life is Beautiful (Benigni), 125
Lifton, Robert Jay, 33–36, 121
limits of representation. *See* unspeakability of trauma
Lin, Maya, 3
Lincoln, Abraham, 99
Listening to Trauma (Caruth), 61
literary scholarship, paradigms in, 45–50, 53–54, 61–62
literary trauma theory, 5–6, 45–50, 66, 71–72
Literature in the Ashes of History (Caruth), 61
Littell, Jonathan, 122
Litz, Brett, 122–23
Long Way Gone, A (Beah), 125
loss, 79, 81
Love's Knowledge (Nussbaum), 54

Luckhurst, Roger, 4, 12, 16, 23–24, 41, 113–14, 136–7
Lumey, L. H., 86
Lyotard, Jean-François, 7, 48–50, 72

MacNair, Rachel, 122
Mallarmé, Stéphane, 68
Marxism, 8, 51
Maus (Spiegelman), 56, 76, 84–85, 89, 92
Maus II (Spiegelman), 84–85
Mazower, Mark, 110
McCarthyism, 42
medico-legal professionals, 15, 17
melancholia, 65, 73, 78–79, 81–82, 136
memory, 4, 10, 22–25, 37, 56–59, 63, 69, 78–79, 84–89, 96, 111, 137–39
Memory and Complicity (Sanyal), 111
mental illness, 28, 31–32
Micale, Mark, 5, 13, 24, 28
Michaels, Anne, 6
microaggressions, 106
Milgram, Stanley, 121
Miller, J. Hillis, 51, 54, 62
Milosevic, Slobodan, 117
modernity, 2, 6–7, 12–16, 28, 43, 49
Morag, Raya, 121
moral injury, 122–23
morality, 119
Morrison, Toni, 5, 56, 83, 114
Moses, 94–96
Moses, A. Dirk, 110
Moses, Citizen & Me (Jarrett-Macauley), 125
Moses and Monotheism (Freud), 24, 27–28, 57, 94–98, 118
mourning, 65, 73, 78–79, 84, 91, 138–39, 141
Mowitt, John, 139–40
Multidirectional Memory (Rothberg), 9, 111
Mumford, Lewis, 127

narrative memory, 58–59, 78–79
national trauma, 99–102
National Wildlife Federation, 130
Nazi Germany, 10, 27, 70, 124
Neal, Arthur, 99
Nelson, Tim Blake, 125
Nemes, László, 125
neo-Nazism, 10
nervous disorders, 12–13, 19
neurasthenia, 14
neurosis, 13–14, 17–18, 26–29, 58, 94
New Criticism, 61–62
Nichols, Jeff, 129
Night (Wiesel), 90
9/11, 1–2, 9, 57, 87, 89, 99, 104, 123, 129
nostalgia, 81–82
Novak, Lorie, 86
Nuremberg trials, 70
Nussbaum, Martha, 53–54

Obama, Barack, 1–2, 10–11
Oedipus complex, 25
Onion, The, 125–26
Oppenheim, Hermann, 14, 17–19, 28–29
Oppenheimer, Joshua, 122
oppression-based trauma, 108–09
original sin, 96
Origins of Totalitarianism, The (Arendt), 110
Owen, Wilfred, 6
Oxford English Dictionary, 2, 43

Page, Herbert, 15
Palimpsestic Memory (Silverman), 111
Parade's End (Ford), 128
Parker, David, 53
Parmesan, Camille, 130
Partition, 104–05
pathological public sphere, 42, 139–40
Pearl Harbor, 99
pedagogy, 68
Pederson, Joshua, 121, 123
people of colour, 105
perpetration-induced traumatic stress (PITS), 122
perpetrators, 82, 104, 117–25
perpetrator trauma, 104, 117–25
Phillips, Caryl, 6

Plath, Sylvia, 92
Poetic Justice (Nussbaum), 54
Poetics (Aristotle), 6
Politics of Friendship, The (Derrida), 54
postcolonial syndrome, 109
Postcolonial Witnessing (Craps), 106
postmemory, 84–87
postmodernism, 49, 114
poststructuralism, 50–51, 53, 80, 113
post-traumatic growth, 136
post-traumatic stress disorder (PTSD): alternatives to, 136–37; definitions of, 4, 7, 55–56, 126–27, 133; limitations of, 108–09; origins of, 33, 35, 119–22
poverty, 16, 87
pre-traumatic stress, 104, 125–31
prosthetic memory, 88–89, 94
psychiatry, 19–21, 23, 28, 34–35, 38–39, 119
psychoanalysis, 19–20, 23–26, 60, 66, 70
psychodynamic, 13, 37, 38

racism, 1–3, 105, 108
Radstone, Susannah, 100, 121, 135
railway and industrial accidents, 7, 14–19, 20, 25, 41, 95
Railway Injuries (Page), 15
railway spine, 14–19, 41
Rankine, Claudia, 105
rape, 37, 39–40
Reader, The (Schlink), 121–22
Reading, Anna, 138–39
Rechtman, Richard, 119–20
reconciliation, 117
re-enactment, 70, 77
Regeneration (Barker), 6
rehabilitation, 30
repetition compulsion, 58, 77, 78
Report of the War Office Committee of Enquiry into 'Shell-Shock', 31
representation, limits of. *See* unspeakability of trauma
repression of memories, 4, 24–25, 27, 138
Requiem for a Nun (Faulkner), 1–2
resilience, 136–37
Rigney, Ann, 139
Road to Yesterday, The (DeMille), 88
Robbins, Bruce, 124
Rorty, Richard, 53
Rose, Gillian, 121
Rose, Jacqueline, 93
Ross, Kristin, 138
Rothberg, Michael, 9, 48, 111, 119, 124, 141–42
Rothe, Anne, 114, 132–33
Rubin, David, 126

safe-world violations, 109
Saint-Amour, Paul, 127–28
Salpêtrière Hospital, 19, 21, 24
Sanyal, Debarati, 111
Sassoon, Siegfried, 6
Saving the Text (Hartman), 62
Schindler's List (Spielberg), 89–91, 125
Schlink, Bernhard, 121–22
Scholar's Tale, A (Hartman), 62
Sebald, W. G., 6, 86, 114
secondary traumatization, 56–57, 68, 76, 83, 87–88
secondary witnessing, 82–83, 90–91, 94
Second World War, 10, 32–34, 42, 45–46, 70, 75, 92, 110
Seiffert, Rachel, 122
Sellin, Ernst, 95
Seltzer, Mark, 7, 42, 139–40
Semelin, Jacques, 110
sexuality and trauma, 24–26
Shatan, Chaim, 33, 35–36
Shay, Jonathan, 122
shell-shock, 6, 14, 31–32, 41, 127
Shoah (Lanzmann), 67, 76, 115
Sicher, Efraim, 94
Silverman, Max, 111
Simpson, O. J., 70
Sin Sick (Pederson), 121, 123
slavery, 2, 5, 9, 57, 87, 88, 104–05
Smelser, Neil, 101
Smethurst, Tobi, 115
social construction of trauma, 14, 28, 43, 98–102

Sokal, Alan, 135
somnambulism, 21–22
Song for Night (Abani), 125
Son of Saul (Nemes), 125
Sontag, Susan, 84
Spec Ops: The Line, 122
spectacle of suffering, 114
Specters of Marx (Derrida), 54
Spiegel, John, 33
Spiegelman, Art, 56, 76, 84–86, 92
Spielberg, Steven, 89–91, 125
Spitzer, Robert, 35
Springer, Jerry, 114
Sri Lanka tsunami, 108
Steiner, George, 7, 46, 50, 72
Stocks, Claire, 40
Stolen Generations, the, 104–05
Stone, Dan, 110
structural trauma, 79–83
Studies on Hysteria (Freud and Breuer), 23–24
subconscious, 22–23, 25
Summerfield, Derek, 107
survivors, 81, 84, 114, 124
Sweig, Arnold, 27
symptoms of trauma, 19–20, 22, 34, 37, 55–56

Taine, Hippolyte, 21
Take Shelter (Nichols), 129
Tal, Kalí, 39
Tasso, Torquato, 106, 117–18
Taylor, Charles (philosopher), 53
Taylor, Charles (politician), 117
Tedeschi, Richard, 137
Tense Future (Saint-Amour), 127–28
testimony, 59, 62, 65–72, 75–76, 81, 90, 106, 118, 135, 140
Testimony (Felman and Laub), 65–72, 75, 115
therapy, 58, 82–83
Three Mile Island, 98
Time's Arrow (Amis), 121–22
Tolstoy, Leo, 71
Tomsky, Terri, 4
Totem and Taboo (Freud), 94–95
transference, 4, 83–87
trauma: aesthetic of, 3, 47–48, 112; canon of, 112–16; community of, 98; culture of, 4, 13, 42, 90, 134, 139; departure from, 80–81; diagnosis of, 28–33, 35–41, 122; economy of, 4; envy of, 140; as a genre, 6, 116; individual and collective, 8, 27, 94–102; industry of, 3–4; and the law, 70–71; in literature, 3, 45–50, 56–57, 59, 67, 71–72, 76, 88–89, 92, 106, 117, 125; in media, 3, 9, 57, 88–89, 100, 115–16, 125; models of, 40–41; narratives of, 129; from oppression, 108–09; re-enactment of, 70; repetition of, 40, 77; responses to, 137; and sexuality, 24–26; social construction of, 14, 28, 43; symptoms of, 19–20, 22, 34, 37, 55–56, 123; terminology of, 2–5, 13, 15–17, 28, 43, 55–56, 107; theories of, 8, 45–50, 52–53, 55–61, 73–104, 109, 112, 114–15, 132–33; transference of, 83–87; treatment of, 29–30, 34, 39, 58, 134; unspeakability of, 6, 46–47, 49, 58–59, 67, 71, 75, 80; valorization of, 4, 42, 77–80, 90, 113, 133, 140
Trauma: A Genealogy (Leys), 133
Trauma Culture (Kaplan), 89
trauma economy, 4
trauma envy, 140
Trauma: Explorations in Memory (Caruth), 55, 74–75, 98, 110
trauma industry, 3–4
Trauma Question, The (Luckhurst), 113
traumatic knowledge, 61–65
traumatic memory, 58
Traumatic Neuroses of War, The (Kardiner), 32
traumatic neurosis, 13, 14, 16, 17–19, 25–27, 29, 32, 58
Traverso, Enzo, 139
treatment of trauma, 29–30, 34, 39, 58, 134
trigger warnings, 68–69

Trimarco, James, 100
Turn of the Screw, The (James), 66
type II traumas, 109

Ulysses (Joyce), 128
Unclaimed Experience (Caruth), 52–53, 55, 60–61, 106, 110
unknowability. *See* unspeakability of trauma
unspeakability of trauma, 6, 46–47, 49, 58–59, 67, 71, 75, 80

valorization of trauma, 4, 77–80, 90, 113, 133
van Alphen, Ernst, 46
van der Hart, Onno, 58
van der Kolk, Bessel, 58, 133
Van Susteren, Lise, 128
Vermeulen, Pieter, 61–62, 64–65
Veterans Administration, 32–36, 38
Veterans Bureau. *See* Veterans Administration
victimhood, 3–4, 82, 120, 123–24, 136, 142
victim-perpetrator binary, 124–25, 142
video games, 114–15
Vietnam veterans, 3, 120
Vietnam War, 33–34, 39, 108
Volger, Thomas, 53
voyeuristic fetishism, 140

Waltzing with Bashir (Morag), 121
Waltz with Bashir (Folman), 122
War Neuroses (Grinker and Spiegel), 33
war neurosis, 14, 28–29, 33, 57
War on Terror, the, 2, 123
wartime experiences, 26, 29, 32, 107
Watters, Ethan, 108
Weilnböck, Harald, 132–34, 136
Weissman, Gary, 90–93
Welzer, Harald, 121
Western-centrism, 37–38, 41, 104–12
Whitehead, Anne, 5
Wiesel, Elie, 67, 90
Wiklormirski, Binjamin, 92
Williams, Serena, 105
Winfrey, Oprah, 114
witnessing, 50, 55, 59–60, 65–72, 75, 82–83, 87–94, 115
Wolmar, Christian, 14–15
Woolf, Virginia, 52
Wordsworth, William, 61–63
Wordsworth's Poetry, 1787–1814 (Hartman), 61
working class, 16, 30
working-through, 73–79, 82
wound culture, 7, 42, 82
Wretched of the Earth, The (Fanon), 109

Yale school, 51–52, 55, 62, 66
Young, Allan, 33, 38, 106

Zidane, Zinedine, 105
Zimbardo, Philip, 121
Zimmerer, Jürgen, 110
Zone of Interest, The (Amis), 125